My Florida

My Florida

By Ernest Lyons

Illustrated by James Hutchinson

South Brunswick and New York:
A. S. Barnes and Company
London: Thomas Yoseloff Ltd

A. S. Barnes and Co., Inc.
Cranbury, New Jersey 08512

Thomas Yoseloff Ltd
18 Charing Cross Road
London W.C. 2, England

SBN 498-07366-1
Printed in the United States of America

To Lyle and Kip

Author's Note

These Florida sketches, revised and with some new material, were gleaned from many appearing as "Ernest Lyons' Column" on the editorial page of *The Stuart* (Fla.) *News.* The News is Scripps–Howard Newspapers' only semi–weekly, publishing Thursdays and Sundays. Stuart, on the St. Lucie River forty miles north of Palm Beach, was the Tom Sawyer town of my boyhood, where I enjoyed Florida as a barefooted kid around 1915–and haven't stopped since. I grew up haunting the docks and fish houses, roaming the rivers and swamps. Let's say that the columns turned into a labor of love, the editor vicariously enjoying the outdoors through his typewriter when he couldn't get there any other way, or recalling when his town–now a bright little city casting a glow in the sky–was a place where the Seminoles used to come in and trade at

My Florida

Uncle Walter Kitching's store.

Our readers seemed to like the columns. *The News* was acquired by Scripps–Howard Newspapers in 1965 and some of the Florida sketches received wide circulation among member newspapers. Walker Stone, editor–in–chief, suggested the book as, perhaps, offering a new viewpoint of Florida. Margaret Wilson helped compile it. I am honored that Jim Hutchinson, who has a real feeling for wilderness Florida, did the illustrations. Stephen Trumbull, who kindly wrote the introduction, was for many years the star Florida feature writer for *The Miami Herald*–but he can whip up a mess of grits, swamp cabbage and fried catfish even better.

My Florida is dedicated to two friends who will be glad to know that I at last made the deadline: Lyle C. Wilson and Willard M. Kiplinger.

—Ernest F. Lyons,
Editor, *The Stuart News*

Contents

Introducing the Columnist

As a recently retired Miami newspaperman whose assignment for many years was the off–beat segments of the state, I first met Ernie Lyons long ago.

I felt a kinship for him on the occasion of that first meeting, a feeling that drew the additional spice of respect and admiration as the years passed.

I found myself reading more and more of his columns and telling myself: "I wish I had written that." And what greater tribute can one newspaperman pay a fellow craftsman?

He had an advantage I always envied. Whereas I had served my apprenticeship in cities like Chicago, Los Angeles and New Orleans—finding that part of Florida the bulldozers had not yet found only when I was quite mature—Ernie had been raised in this setting.

He and his father—who also must have been quite a

11

guy—had camped in those piney flatwoods and explored those lakes and rivers when Ernie was just a boy. He grew up to be as much a part of the scene as the gopher turtles, the raccoons and 'possums, the palmetto clumps and the cabbage palms which he loves.

His big mistake was becoming a newspaper reporter on the home town sheet back in the Big Depression "because," as he told me, "I just couldn't make a living rowing to the inlet and back when the price of sea trout dropped to two cents a pound."

I suspect that he had never hit a lick of indoor work until then, but Ernie had a knack of knowing how words should be put together. He knew his community, its possibilities and its foibles. Almost before the fishline cuts had healed on his hands, he became editor of the small weekly.

He edited with everything in him—right up to the minute the paper went to press. Then he was off for his beloved back country and his woodsy and sometimes unwashed friends there.

But in his working hours he started to accumulate a collection of awards and press association trophies for his paper, a collection that now has reached truly formidable proportions. The outer office has a big cabinet so full of them it looks like a case at the Smithsonian Institution.

He has won many "Best Original Column" state awards, "Best Editorial" awards and just about every honor the Florida newspaper fraternity has to bestow. He does not have any award from the U.S. Engineer Corps, whom he has tagged as "The River Killers" because of what they have done to Florida's streams with their dredges.

You'll find Ernie at the desk that has all the fishing tackle on it. You may find some weatherbeaten old character—who may be wearing unaccustomed shoes out of deference to a first trip to town in months—talking sincerely with him.

I think you will like *My Florida*. If you want to see some still—unspoiled sections of the state—while avoiding the clip joints and tourist traps—you will love it.

His is a gentle, down-to-earth approach, warm and understanding. He writes, not of "them," but of "us."

You will not meet many of Florida's sacred cows in his book. You will meet far more shantyboat and woodlands shack dwellers, some of whom are probably happy that Ernie found them before the sheriff did.

I am happy that he is out to perpetuate a portion of Florida which we both sadly know is on its way out.

—Steve Trumbull

Introducing the Artist

James Hutchinson, illustrator of this book, acquired his deep sense of Florida's cypress swamps and cabbage palm hammocks by literally living with the Indians. These drawings, two of which are of the Seminoles and the rest on wilderness, pioneer and wildlife themes, show his love for "the real Florida" to which he has been so close. One of the few white men accepted by the tribe, the artist has spent an average of three and one–half months a year for the past eight years in the Everglades with the Seminoles. He has a permanent camp at the Brighton Reservation. Hutchinson's Seminole paintings were exhibited by the U.S. Army in 1957 at the Berlin Folk Festival. They were featured in "The American Artist" in 1965. He was the first artist to hold an exhibition at Florida State Museum.

In an introduction to "Seminoles of Florida," a catalog of Hutchinson's Seminole Indian paintings, noted Florida writer Theodore Pratt, author of *The Barefoot*

Mailman and many other books, wrote:

"I first met young Jim Hutchinson of Port Salerno, Florida, about eight years ago when he painted the first of his Seminole Indian works. I knew something of the subject, having written a novel about them, *Seminole,* but it took no great discernment to see that here was a true and real artist who has a special feeling for Florida's Indians. I told him then that if he made a good part of his life career painting the Seminoles he could go down with the greatest of American Indian painters such as Catlin, Remington and the others.

"Since then Hutchinson has painted over 500 Seminole works, which now sell for appreciable prices, and he is becoming known nationally for this. Some of it was exhibited at the New York World's Fair.

"One reason it is so good, apart from his exceptional talent, is that Hutchinson has taken the trouble to know what he is painting. With his wife Joan he has gone for extended periods to camp and lived with the Seminoles on their reservations, getting to know and observe them at first hand. I have visited the Hutchinsons when they lived and he worked on the Brighton Reservation. When he painted there (several times) the famous late Seminole patriarch, Billy Bowlegs, he was painting a friend whose chickee was near where he camped.

"He caught Billy while still alive in his nineties, just in time. He is also catching, no more than in time, the true flavor of the unique, colorful old time Seminole customs and costumes. And in doing this he is doing more than painting the Indians of his state; he is painting Florida, for Seminole and Florida history are inseparable. In this way Jim Hutchinson is one of the greatest artistic assets Florida possesses. Any time now substitute 'United States' for Florida."

My Florida

1

My Florida Is Different From Some Floridas

My Florida is the inundated prairie dotted by lonesome cabbage palm hammocks, cypress islands and bayheads, with an undulating flock of egrets like galloping white horses in the distance. It is the ground owl and the caracara.

My Florida is the pine, palmetto and wire grass woods, where the bees go from the penny-royal to the wild honeysuckle and the placid gopher tortoise walks rocking on its stubby legs, stretching out time.

My Florida is the little spruce trees on the white sugar sand of their rolling dunes, all leaning the way the wind has bent them, with the gray-green lichens below and the nests of flying squirrels in their branches. It is scrub-oaks covered with orange love-vines and a saucy towhee scratching.

It is not a well-manicured green lawn joining on to the lawn of a neighbor, and then more lawns joining lawns, all neat and orderly and characterless.

My Florida is winding sand trails where you still see turkey, deer and wild hog tracks. It is something I saw the other morning: a beautiful buck leaping effortlessly up over a barbed wire fence and bounding off with his white flag flying. Thence came the pioneer expression: "He high-tailed it out of there."

It is not the supermarket parking lot.

My Florida is the winding tropical river, heavy with the musky scent of palm blossoms, with water turkeys sunning themselves, striped necked turtles plopping from logs, grey squirrels barking and the rat-tat-tat of the pileated woodpecked resounding.

It is not a CBS, all-electric Medallion home.

My Florida is the tarpon rolling, the mullet leaping for fun, pelicans diving, red-beaked skimmer gulls skimming the surface with their bills, a manatee blowing, and an eagle stealing a fish from an osprey high in air.

It is not a four-lane highway.

My Florida is the strangling fig tree swallowing a palm, shoestring ferns in the hammock's shade, wild orchids, spanish moss and crimson-flowered airplants.

It is not a Washingtonia palm tree in a park planting, or a hibiscus bush.

My Florida is cruising offshore in a small boat just as the sun comes up, grabbing a bending rod and boating a king mackerel, watching sea turtles and manta rays, coming back in through a boisterous inlet "on a wing and a prayer."

It is not playing shuffleboard.

My Florida is wading a sand-bottomed backwoods

pond, flycasting a cork-bodied bug on a well greased GAF line, catching three or four "yearling-and-up" bass, enjoying their beauty and liking their musky smell—and then eating them fried to a tasty brown by the pond side.

It is not a Royal Castle hamburger or a Lum's frankfurter.

My Florida is Quahog clams from Sebastian, squirt clams from those few places where some are left around the inlet, cup oysters from Peck's Lake, a fresh caught pompano from the beach, bluefish caught in the afternoon and broiled that night, and fresh grouper fingers from one I caught myself down by the Hole.

It is not that most dreadful of dreadfuls, bakery made Key lime pie.

My Florida is shredded swamp cabbage cut by the creek, with only the sweet and no bitter, steamed in a Dutch oven with some fried salt pork and a few sliced onions, served with hush-puppies (white corn meal), fried bream and willow cats, topped off with black coffee boiled with a stick across the top of the pot.

It is not a slice of sweet canned pineapple with cottage cheese in the middle.

My Florida is squatty custard apple trees and moon vines—and "watch out for that moccasin!" It is mean old hermits willing to cut one guy and give the next the last pull on the jug. It is hauling up sheepshead from under the mangroves and watching Ma Coon take the younkers for a stroll on an oyster bar in the twilight.

It is not pink-kneed vacationers in sun glasses and

Bermuda shorts.

My Florida is surf casting from the sea beach with no one in sight a mile either way.

It is not taking a dip in a swimming pool, covering yourself with lotion and sunbathing in a reclining chair.

My Florida is going fast.

2

Memory of Some Happy
Seminoles in Early Morning

There is a beautiful painting in my mind. It is a treasure of my heart. Every so often it comes back to me: the morning that I saw the happy Seminoles.

We saw a good many Seminoles in Stuart's early days. But they never did strike me as being happy. They would come into town to trade 'coon hides and otter pelts for staples at Uncle Walter Kitching's big store.

The bucks did all the trading, although the squaws indicated what they wanted. When they bought, it was one item at a time. There was always a gulf. It was apparent that they did not trust the white man, not even their good friend "Kitchee" or his son-in-law John Taylor. Part way, yes, but not far.

The squaws and pickaninnies—that's what the early residents called the children—would go house to house selling blueberries for ten cents a basket. The trade

wasn't very smart because some folks started the rumor that they weren't really blueberries but pokeberries which could poison you. That wasn't true, but it showed the mutual distrust.

Along about the beginning of hunting season in the fall, the word would circulate that the Indians were coming in to kill all the deer and turkeys and grab off all the 'coons and otter in the backwoods before the white folks could get them. That was before they had penned up the Indians at Brighton, Big Cypress and Dania, long before there was a barbed wire fence between Stuart and Lake Okeechobee.

All the Indians I had ever seen were glum, morose and distrustful. The women were loaded with rainbow dresses and petticoats that swept the ground, strings of turquoise beads up to their chins, and they all looked like they needed baths. They were barefooted. The men wore rainbow shirts down to their knees, sort of like Greek kilts, their legs were scarred and their bare feet as calloused as an alligator's back leather.

It had never dawned on me that we white folks were the cause of the Seminoles' unhappiness. I just took it for granted that they were born that way. But one fall Old Man Roebuck and Jesse Baker got up a hunting and trapping party to go out into the Allapattah Flats and beat the darned Indians to the venison and the fur, and I was lucky enough to be invited along although I was only fourteen.

Early one morning I left camp out at Tom Tiger Tail Hammock with my shotgun and my old Walker foxhound Jack. I guess we were hunting just about anything that would move when we came to a place where Tom Tiger Tail Trail crossed a slough about an eighth of a mile wide at a place known as "the Indian Crossing."

Jack and I crouched down in the palmettos, looking out at the the still water. The early rays of the sun were painting golden yellow the trunks of the giant yellow pines across the way. The slough with its borders of saw grass, its margins of bayheads, was as still as polished black glass.

Then, of a sudden, exploding into the water on the far side, came a pack of dogs of all descriptions—big dogs, little dogs, hounds, mongrels, hog-catchers—all swimming our way. Bursting behind them came a dozen ponies ridden by brown-naked Indian boys, laughing and yelling.

Next, sloshing through the water on horseback, came the bucks in their rainbow shirts with rifles and shotguns, and then the little gypsy caravan wagons carrying the squaws, old men and old women—and, of course, the furs they were bringing in to "Kitchee."

They were happy. The whole darned crowd was as happy as carefree gypsies on the move. Then I stood up, Jack growled at the Indian dogs and they growled and snarled back, and the whole caravan turned glum.

I had a few dollars with which I tried to buy some 'coon hides, but it was no dice. I was the fly in their soup, the hated white man, a member of the distrusted race. They went on and made camp somewhere, started a big forest fire which burned out our camp, and Old Man Roebuck went down wind of them and set a fire that burned them out. "If those darned Indians want fire, I'll give 'em fire," he said.

It was a long time ago, but at least I saw some happy Seminoles—happy till they saw me.

3

A Supper Reading in a Real Fine Home on River's Shore

Every so often, when I see $50,000 homes and two-car garages along the river bank, with snazzy cruisers tied to the docks, I am reminded of the suppers which I used to share occasionally in one of the first homes on the far side of the St. Lucie River.

The father of the house was a Florida Cracker, called back then a "mullet-choker," which meant that he was a gill-net fisherman for mullet. Every night he would set out his linen nets to drift slowly up and down the river with the tide while some hapless mullet, never too many, got caught by the gills in the meshes.

Mullet were bringing two cents a pound. It was depression and the cheapest grade of salt pork, called "sow bosom with the buttons," retailed for a nickel a pound. My friend did all right in those hard times. Some nights he might make fifty cents or a dollar and occasionally he hit it rich, coming in with a skiff-load of mullet worth as much as ten bucks—and that was when the fish house took out eight dollars to apply on the cost of the net.

He never complained and he did right well. Of course, he didn't have the money to buy false teeth and he had a pair of mail-order glasses that weren't much better than nothing although they helped a little mending broken meshes. He had a fine house and six children and a passel of dogs and a cat or two, a flock of free-roaming chickens and a good wife. The only sort of clothes I ever saw him wear were much washed, bleached-out overalls with a faded blue shirt and a straw hat for week days and a black felt hat and a white shirt for Sundays.

The old lady and the girls did right well, too, because he was a considerate father, and saw that the flour and the chicken feed were bought in sacks made of printed dress material. They always had nice dresses made from the flour and feed sacks which featured floral patterns, and the little boys wore the same fancy sort of overalls that their Daddy did. There was an iron wash pot in the yard and always wash on the line, a credit I thought to the wife and mother.

They had a real fine home made out of cabbage palm log posts, tightly thatched with palm fronds on the roof and sides. The floor was dirt, always cleanly swept, and the furnishings were good, simple stuff made out of old packing boxes and driftwood and odds and ends that my friend picked up along the beaches. I don't know where he got them, but he had plenty of real chairs of various sizes and shapes, including two willow rockers, and a couple of top-notch coal oil lamps.

The interior of the home was partitioned into three sections by dividers made of burlap sacks sewn together: a dining room, a bedroom for Pa and Ma, and a bedroom for the kids. There wasn't any kitchen because they cooked in the yard out in the open most of the time or under an old canvas fly when it rained. My friend was a good provider and the soul of hospitality. If I happened to be passing that way toward evening, walking in from fishing or hunting, he would hail me and insist that I stay and have supper with them. "Always a God's plenty for everybody," he would say.

Frankly, I enjoyed those visits, because I realized that my friend was blessed, making the most of Nature's bounty. I knew that he had a good job, drifting that shirt tail of a gill-net for the river to pour its bounty into, and it was plain to see that he was independent as a hog on ice, if he just didn't owe the fish house for the net.

Grits were cheap and so was salt pork and there was always plenty of mullet. When stormy periods came around and he could not get out on the river, he would go catch a couple of soft shelled turtles and the Old Lady would make up a marvelous turtle stew, or he would go out with his long prod-pole and jerk some gopher tortoises out of their holes, or they would even kill a chicken as a last resort.

They ate real well and she set a fine table. It might be that old standby, fried mullet and grits, with crisp salt pork on the side and pork gravy for the grits; or a pilau made of rice and the marsh birds that are so rigorously protected today; and always there was hot bread made in the dutch oven set off to one side of the coals.

My friend was bounteously blessed and he knew that he was. When we all sat down to supper in the various shaped chairs around the packing box table with the two coal oil lamps burning brightly, the little boys in the clean overalls and the little girls in their clean dresses, the Old Man—I guess he was knocking on forty—would put on his mail-order spectacles, flip open an ancient giant-sized family Bible, affix a verse with his finger and give us a supper reading. They were his specialty.

We bowed our heads while he slowly read, although he did not utter a word. I sneaked a peek one time and saw that his lips were moving and a gnarled forefinger was slowly going down the lines. After he was finished, he would put the Bible in front of his oldest daughter—she was twelve and going to school in town—show her the line where he had started and the line where he had ended, and she would read it aloud to us.

We got a wonderful variety. Sometimes it was out of Psalms or Deuteronomy or Numbers or Genesis—wherever the moving finger went—always chanted in the sing-song voice of a recitation and with much stumbling and fumbling over the hard words. Once she asked Papa how to pronounce Nebuchadnezzar, slowly spelling it to him, but he told her she'd never learn if she didn't stick to it on her own.

The real fine home of palmetto thatch has long ago vanished, the old mullet-choker and his helpmate are long gathered back to the fold and the children are scattered afar. All I know of have turned out pretty good. Sometimes when I see the people living in their $50,000 houses with their gleaming cars and bright cruisers and all the evidence of material prosperity upon the river bank, I wonder:

"But did you ever sit down to a supper reading from a man who couldn't read or write?"

4

Moonshine and Pancakes
in an Old Boar's Nest

The most interesting people I know are hermits who
live in boar's nests, although some of them are a little
peculiar.

There was Old Baldy who lived in a wrecked boat
under the Australian pines at the south side of St.
Lucie Inlet. The boat had been cast ashore in a
hurricane and he fixed it up ship-shape as a real, fine
home. Hermits are not messy as most people think, but
keep everything tidy and in its place.

Old Baldy had his pans hung on neat pegs on the
trees all around his outdoor fireplace. He always washed
his dish cloth and hung it up to dry. He was friendlier
than some hermits who have the habit of coming out of
their hidey-holes and yelling: "Go away! You're
trespassing!"

One morning my boat broke down near Old Baldy's
hideaway and he asked me over to breakfast. I accepted

and sat by the coals. "What are we having for breakfast?" I asked.

"Moonshine and pancakes," he replied. "Isn't that what everybody has for breakfast?" Like I said, some are peculiar.

Another one I knew was named Joe; I never did learn his last name. He lived in a beautiful sort of an eagle's nest home that he had built on top of three cypress stumps in a swamp near Lake Helen Blazes in the St. Johns Marsh. The house was made out of old drift boards and pieces of sheet metal that Joe had salvaged somewhere. A proper boar's nest should not cost more than a dime, if you don't count the nails and baling wire that it takes to hold it together.

Joe's house even had a front porch that leaned crazily. He cooked on the front porch in a sand box and for furniture he had an old patched-up rocker and a real swell settee made out of the front seat of a junked automobile.

I ran into Joe on a bass fishing trip. He was the youngest hermit I ever knew and had a most interesting story. Seems like he had worked real hard as a ranch hand and a catfish fisherman and a frogger until he got disgusted with work.

"I decided on my 24th birthday never to hit another lick so long as I lived," he told me. "I'm a free man. I don't bass-guide, I don't mend somebody else's fences, I don't frog and if it wasn't for my darned stomach I wouldn't even run a catfish trotline."

It bothered Joe that he had to catch a few catfish, take them to town and sell them for enough to buy grits and bacon. That was in the thirties and I can't help but think how happy Joe would be if he was hermiting today and had a nice little welfare check coming in to lick the stomach problem.

Some hermits are born out of their time and would have made good pirates a couple of centuries ago. One of these was Old Hookey who had a wonderful hermitage alongside a huge sawdust pile way up the North Fork near a clear little creek.

Old Hookey ran a small industry on the side manufacturing snake bite medicine in a bayhead at the head of the little creek. He didn't enjoy doing anything unless it was illegal and then he considered it fun, not work. He really lived high on the hog, although it was usually somebody else's hog.

One time he invited me up to his place and he was real proud of the fact that he had somehow gotten a 200-pound block of ice up there and buried it in the sawdust pile. He bragged he had "real refrigeration," something enjoyed by very few hermits. Hermits are snobs like all of us.

He asked how would I like some fried fish for supper and I said that sounded real good. He cut off a bush, got his spear and sneaked down to the creek bank pushing the bush ahead of him like an Indian. Pretty soon the spear flashed and he came out with a six-pound black bass.

"Don't you know that's illegal," I told him. "Sure," he said. "That makes them taste better."

The big hazard that hermits face is being run off their properties by whoever is paying the taxes. The happiest one I ever knew made a deal with the land owner to run other people off. When he yelled: "Go

away! You're trespassing!" he had a paper to back it up
and could shoot you if he wanted. Anyhow, that's what
he told me and I believed him.

5

People, Known and Unknown, Along the River

There are people known and people heard about along the river. The line is thin. In time, the mind accepts both the real and the imaginary and you are apt to feel you know the one as well as the other.

One I knew well was Lou Hitchcock, the skinny, red-headed Irish dreamer who was determined to be rich. Lou and his woman— he called her Baby—lived in a shack of bleached driftwood down by the Hole in the Wall where the St. Lucie goes to sea. They subsisted on fried fish and grits, with a can of beans or so and a little tobacco for Lou. Occasionally he would trade some fish for a fruit jar of white whiskey and the woman hated him for it.

I got to knowing them when I ventured into the Hole to dig the wonderful squirt clams that were abundant in those days before the channel through to the Steamboat Passage filled in. Lou cottoned to me

41

and let me in on his secret hopes and dreams. He was squatting on a piece of oceanfront land and was going to be rich, rich, rich!

With the sandflies and the mosquitoes eating at us like a burning plague, we would squat around a smudge fire in the evening with a bucket of steamed clams nearby. Lou would take a sip out of the fruit jar and say to the woman:

"We're going to be big rich. Stick with me, Baby, and you'll be wearing diamonds on all your fingers. I'm going to be a millionaire. We'll sail by here in our fancy yacht drinking champagne. You'll have servants waiting on you, Baby, caring for your every need."

Baby was growing old before her time. Her hair was a rat's nest. The sun and the wind had turned her face to wrinkled leather—but you could tell by her eyes as she listened that she half-way wanted to believe.

"You can even have your own beautician on the yacht," Lou promised, taking another sip. That was too much for Baby.

"You and your God-damned promises!" she spat.

"You're no damned good and you never will be. I'm tired of being eaten by these infernal sandflies. I'm sick of drinking this puking brackish water. I hate fish and I hate beans. You won't make nobody rich," she said, "because that God-damned moonshine will kill you in the end."

It was very embarrassing to me. Lou was embarrassed, too, and he tried to cover up by turning to me. "Drink some more of that clam juice young fellow, it'll put hair on your chest."

I wondered why the clam juice hadn't put any hair

on his chest. Lou was thin as a plucked heron. He worked so hard. Every day he would row over to the homestead where he was squatting on the ocean beach. He had heard that if you cleared a piece and built a house on it and lived there for seven years it was yours.

With his pants cut off at the knees, bare-legged and bare-footed, shirtless, freckled as a toadfish, streaming sweat, he would hack and hack at the palmettos and the mangroves. Sometimes I would pass down the beach and just see the curved blade of his brush-axe at its apogee as he raised it to slash down, hacking away at the jungle that was going to make him rich.

He told Baby that he was going to build a fine home of real lumber, not driftwood, on it, and some day the rich people would come along and buy the oceanfront for resorts and estates.

As a matter of fact, they did. The last I heard of the land, it sold for $4,000,000.

Lou didn't get any of it. Baby was right. He used to catch a few fish on handlines, mostly sea trout, when he could spare the time, and he would row into Port Salerno to trade them for the necessities.

He would get salt, tobacco and grits, some sow bosom and lard to fry the fish in, and occasionally he would bring back a couple of gallon jugs of fresh water so Baby would not have to scrape a hole in the damp sand and drink brackish water like the 'coons did.

He was always very thoughtful of her. But the last time he didn't quite make it. A blow came up and he fell out of the skiff just off the Hole in the Wall. It had two cans of beans in it, two gallons of fresh water for Baby, and an empty fruit jar.

Lou was real. There are others who seem about as real. I never pass the little cove down by the House of Refuge without seeing Portuguese Joe. He was a Cuban refugee and the only resident of our part of Florida in 1870. I can see him in my mind, hoeing his little Indian pumpkin patch near Lou's clearing, rowing out to greet the few sailing craft that passed by, trading a green turtle for tobacco or flour. He never got rich either, but he lived a life, and the last that is known of him was that he was found floating in the river with his head chopped off.

The spirits of the Tequestas still haunt the strip of land that gave refuge to Portuguese Joe and hope to Lou Hitchcock. Their cracked pottery is underfoot. They were brown and simple people who worshiped the sun. I have closed my eyes and seen them dancing around a painted pole on the hammocks by the sea. It is hard to realize that they have been gone for hundreds of years.

To me the old abandoned homesteads of the pioneers, the long relinquished pineapple plantings, the places where men and women loved and labored, where children played, which were finally taken over again by the jungle, are still peopled.

I can close my eyes and see one serene old man with a flowing white beard, still at an abandoned planting up Winters Creek. After his supper, he goes to a well, pumps a dipper of water, drinks it and then goes walking down a path in the cool of the day. I wonder who he is.

6

Nobody's Going to Need Fatwood Like the Pioneers

The last thing taken from the southern forests is the bones of the ancestors.

Where virgin forests of yellow pine once stood, carpeting the ground with their needles—giant trees in which eagles nested and where fox squirrels played—the stump pullers grunt.

They heave out the resinous roots of trees cut 40 years ago and toss them in tangled piles to be trucked to the railroad. Along with the roots go the pitch-petrified trunks and limbs of fallen trees that were here when the Seminoles roamed.

Pitch-pine, called lighter-knots or fatwood, was one of the blessings of pioneer Florida. Wherever you roamed the flatwoods, there was an abundant supply lying on top of the ground. Cut into small chips and chunks, it served as a cooking fire and the big limbs kept you warm all night when the blue northers blew.

At the camps of the nomadic Seminoles, scattered all

45

through the Allapattah Flats and into Hungry Land, there were always the remnants of the wagon-spoke campfires of the tribe. They would take eight or ten long pitch-pine poles and arrange them in a circle pointing in to the hub. Where the points met was their cooking fire and all it took to replenish it was to push a few spokes inward.

The pitch-pine fence posts of most Florida ranches are semi-straight limbs of trees from another century. There will be no more when they are gone. Creosote-impregnated cypress posts are now taking their place in most new fencings.

Pitch-pine may not last forever, but local surveyors can take you to a remote slough in western Martin County where a federal survey crew planted a fatwood marker more than 100 years ago.

Like coal, pitch-pine stores the golden light of the sun in some magic way not understood by men. It is shipped from here to mills where the resins are extracted and turned into gunpowder, turpentine, medicines, paint ingredients and hundreds of other by-products.

There was a day when the "naval stores industry," as it was then called, was an important part of the economy of this part of Florida. Before the pines were cut, they were bled at their bases. The huge mill at Sherman, the vanished town between Indiantown and Okeechobee City, shipped thousands of barrels of resin gathered from little clay pots attached to the wounded trunks of countless pines.

There's nothing like the fragrant smell of burning pitch-pine, mixed with the aroma of frying fish, simmering fox squirrel and bubbling swamp cabbage or grits. True, you came in from the woods so blackened up that it took hearty scrubbing with good old Fels Naphtha to clean up again—but you had a wonderful time. Pitch-pine was an important part of it.

The woods full of pitch-pine gave the woods roamer a sense of security. There was fuel always at hand. I still can't get over the modern campers who use portable gas and gasoline stoves to cook on. They may be cleaner but they're not half the fun. Cost money to operate, too.

The other afternoon I was out toward the Dunklin Camp on Martin Grade where the citrus groves and the improved pastures are replacing the flatwoods. I looked out over several hundred acres where the palmettos had been gathered and burned and where huge tangled piles of pitch-pine stumps, roots and limbs were gathered waiting to be trucked to the railroad.

"They ought not to do that," I kept saying to myself. "Somebody's going to need that fatwood some day to make a fire to fry some fish or to stay warm through a night."

But I was wrong. Nobody is going to need it any more.

7

How a Pet Coon Brought Grief to a Moral Man

John Hazelwood, the resident trapper of our town's early days, was a moral man and a religious man. He lived with his wife in a trim little white house and they were both neat, respectable people. The house was prim as a parsonage.

Every fall, after the cool weather set in, despite being in his late sixties, Mr. Hazelwood would take his houseboat launch trailing a flat bottomed bateau and head up the North Fork of the St. Lucie.

He stayed out about ten days at a time, always returning with a treasure of squared-out 'coon hides and otter pelts encased on long boards. He returned from one expedition with a lively little kit 'coon that he kept for a pet. Mrs. Hazelwood did not like it one bit because it messed up the house, broke tea cups and got into everything.

But John had a quirk about that 'coon. He was

determined to keep it and keep it he did. He even trained it to use the bathroom and flush the toilet, which ought to have calmed down Mrs. Hazelwood, but she kept picking away at him to take it back where he got it. John was bullheaded. He named the 'coon Robert, which he shortened to Robbie, and everywhere John went Robbie tagged along with that peculiar, loping shuffle of "the little bear with a mask."

As a youngster, I was always making friends with old men around town who knew more about nature and things than I did. I haunted the house of the venerable, white bearded Judge J. B. Adams, who had Ditmar's *Book of Reptiles* and Jordan's *Book of Fishes*—and lots more. In his eighties, Judge Adams decided to stuff every species of fish and to put away in formaldehyde every reptile in this part of Florida.

He was not a very good fish stuffer, but he liked his work and had hundreds of stuffed fish in various stages of odoriferousness mounted on the walls of his living room and kitchen. What an enchanting smell! And there were jars upon jars holding pickled coral snakes, harlequins, puff adders and moccasins.

The Judge was a source of revenue for us youngsters, a coral snake being worth a dime and a good big rattler a quarter. I learned all about fish and reptiles from him, but then I had to go spoil it by asking why he thought God made all those things. "Show me God," he said. "I thought you had some sense."

Mr. Hazelwood taught me about the animals. I would go around his house and fall victim to Robbie's latest trick, which was to perch inside the transom of the front door, land on your neck and take possession.

Robbie had grown into a husky boar 'coon—he must have weighed fifteen pounds—and the sensation of having him take over was anything but comfortable.

"Don't move," Mr. Hazelwood would warn, "and Robbie won't bite you. Just stand still." So I would stand and Robbie would take everything out of my pockets and pick at the pearl buttons on my shirt. "That Robbie!" Mr. Hazelwood would chuckle.

Then he would tell me how 'coons are mischievous and curious, which is often their undoing. "Put a piece of bright mussel shell by a trap and they can't resist it," he said.

He knew all their ways and habits, what they ate, like crawfish and palm berries, and their weaknesses, too. "They're just like people," he said, "they'll take the easy way every time. If you find where they're using, just block off all the other pathways with palm fronds and leave an easy way for your trap to nip their toes."

Then, since I hadn't yet learned that there's nothing immoral about anything where money is concerned, I asked: "But do you think it's RIGHT to take their skins and sell them?" It was sure a boob question.

Mrs. Hazelwood, who had been sweeping so energetically that I suspected she was mentally sweeping us all out, stopped, leaned on her broom and looked at him. He seemed to be speaking both to his wife and to me when he said: "The Lord God Almighty gave man dominion over all creatures. Don't you know your Bible?"

Well, I never felt welcome at his house again. I got to exploring the upper river by boat and once in a while I would see him in his houseboat and envy him. Robbie was always prowling around the boat, a real big, fat prime 'coon whose hide was worth at least three dollars in St. Louis.

But one morning I heard Mr. Hazelwood plaintively calling "Robbie! Oh, Robbie!" and stopped to see if I could help. He was such a neat little man, but when he showed up on the bank he was muddy, tattered and bramble-torn.

"Robbie ran away," he said. "I'll never see him again." He was crying. Losing Robbie just about broke his heart. He never trapped any more.

So I guess there are some things man does not have dominion over.

8

A Mean Old Sow with a Can in Her Mouth Got Help

A friend of mine told me a story I liked the other day. It was a simple little tale which was handed on to him by a barber at Okeechobee City, but to me it illustrates the inherent decency in the average guy.

This man was cane pole fishing with his family over around Fish Eating Creek, that dark little stream which meanders through the cypresses into the northwest corner of Lake Okeechobee, when a gaunt old sow and her litter of pigs came into the clearing. He observed that the sow had a tin can stuck in her mouth, so securely pierced by her teeth that it was a certainty she would starve to death. The pigs were starving, too.

The man made several approaches toward the hog, but found that she was so belligerently protective of her skinny little piglets that he didn't stand a chance of removing that can. Another fishing family pulled up in a car and he approached the driver. "Stranger," he said, "how would you like to help me catch a hog?"

Now catching a full grown, mean, wild and sore woods-roaming hog with a couple of dogs on each ear is no great shakes, but doing it by hand is another matter Those two men chased that hog all over the swamp, with her snorting and the pigs squealing, finally tackled it football fashion, brought it down—and took that can out. "She didn't say thanks," the barber said, "but you never saw a critter eat more grass and leaves faster."

I suppose it would have made a good story with an Androcles and the Lion twist if the sow had let the man take the can without resistance. Anybody who thinks that might have happened doesn't know hogs.

Still, not all animal behavior is predictable. Most redwinged blackbirds fly north about this time of the year to raise their young, but the other day I found three redwing nests in the bulrushes along a west county drainage canal. It is apparent that a good many redwings must nest right here in Florida.

So do quite a few mallards. I'm not talking about the black mallard, which is a native Florida duck, but the same sort of mallards which migrate in great numbers down the Mississippi Valley each fall and back as far north as Canada in the spring.

I know where at least one pair of mallards has a brood of a dozen fuzzy little Floridians because I watched them on a quiet, hidden piece of water last Saturday afternoon.

One of the most graceful and beautiful of all Florida birds is the purple gallinule, which loves lilypad-studded Florida waters. This colorful little rail actually walks from lilypad to lilypad without getting its feet wet.

Recognized naturalists say that it is one of the few birds with a sense of the beauty of flowers. The male bird has been observed carrying a flower in its beak to its mate on the nest.

The bower bird of New Guinea also has a sense of beauty, only in his case he goes for colored pebbles and stones. The male bird builds a hidden nest or bower, then collects smooth, colored rocks which he stores there. He brings his prospective mate around and shows her the loot. If it suits her fancy, she accepts his proposal. Diamonds are a girl's best friend in the bird world, too.

They say that the female of the species has the most protective urge—but it is the male black bass that chases marauders away from the nest, the male sea horse that broods the eggs and hatches the young, and the male gaff-topsail catfish that carries the eggs around in his mouth until they incubate, foregoing food in the hatching period.

Don't bet on what an animal will do. They are individuals and some are "a heck of a lot more individual" than others. We used to have a coal black cat that loved to swim. I went down to the river one night with a gas lantern to spear some flounder. As I waded along in water one foot deep, searching the circle of light for flatfish, I noticed Blackie swimming along behind, keeping me company.

You could put a fresh-caught mullet in a bucket of water and Blackie would plunge in head first and come out dripping wet with the mullet in his teeth. He grew into a fierce, mean tomcat with a swaggering walk, but even in his old age he liked to go down to the river, jump in and cool off.

My dog, Pudge, likes the water, too—but is afraid of rain. Pudge will jump into any lake, pond or river and cavort like a seal, but just let a few drops of rain fall and Pudge whines and whimpers at the back door. Go under the house? Oh, no! A cloudburst can fall and the poor, pitiful dog will stand soaked, shivering and crying its heart out at the cruelties of man. I don't need to read the morning paper for the weather. If the dog is under the bed and has to be put outside by brute force, it means that there are going to be clouds and possible showers.

We had a bobtailed cat once that liked sweet corn on the cob. Pudge demands a slice of watermelon just like the rest of us when we split a melon in the patio. Eats it right down to the rind, too. What does your dog do?

9

The Old Fish House Was a Hangout for Males Only

Like the long house of the Iroquois and the taboo-protected sacred houses on stilts of the head-hunting Dyaks and many Polynesian tribes, the fish houses that once were a normal feature of the shorelines along the Indian and St. Lucie Rivers were strictly male territory.

Port Salerno still has a few left, actively engaged in the fascinating business of icing down and rushing freshly caught fish to market. The old Langberg fish house, one of the last of the real oldtimers, still stoutly stands on the Indian River shore at Sewalls Point, a historic relic which has come through all the hurricanes. The empty old house on barnacled pilings, with its bare mangrove net racks alongside, could tell many a story of rugged men in an era that has passed.

Once Stuart itself was a bustling center of the commerical fishing industry. Fleets of outside handliners and gill-net boats used to unload thousands of pounds of Spanish mackerel, blues and king mackerel daily at the old E. J. Ricou fish house at the foot of N. Colorado Avenue, then called Belle Flora.

Hundreds of thousands of pounds of mullet, bottomfish and fancy fish, such as sea trout, were routed through the C. D. Blakeslee fish house in Stuart just to the east of where the Youth Center stands. In place of today's packaged flowers on the express shed platform downtown were stacked iced barrels of fish and an occasional 300-pounds or better jewfish with a routing tag tied to its gills.

There was Ernest Ricou's huge fish house at Jensen Beach, which handled millions of pounds of seafood before it fell victim to a hurricane, and J. J. Pitchford and Sons handled their share, as did the Glass fish house at Rio.

All the old fish houses had one thing in common; they were strictly a man's world. Some had marathon poker games going on when weather fouled up the fishing and some of the fishermen could outdrink and outcurse the most accomplished Barbary pirates.

While they were in the towns, they were not of the towns, but separate—with an unwritten law that only a few beside the regular net crews were welcome in them. No exclusive club was ever more selective in who could sit in on a poker game. A derelict might find a hearty welcome and a hand-out in one while a leading citizen of the town might get cussed out and told to get going.

Night and day, year in and year out, the old fish houses along the river—now blown into fading memory by the great winds and the changing times—were the clubhouses of an independent male fraternity.

And what rugged characters some of them were! I remember one short, barrel shaped fisherman in knee boots who bragged that he could not remember ever taking a bath. There exuded from him an odor of fish so powerful that he enjoyed the ultimate in privacy. He could walk into any store in town and people would give him fifteen to twenty feet clearance.

Some were as fine square shooters as I have ever met. Once you were accepted as a friend, they would share meals, money, fish and anything else they had. A few were erratic characters, quick to pick a quarrel—and better stayed away from.

During the Great Depression, hundreds of hungry people would line up with sacks, boxes, baskets and newspapers at the old Blakeslee fish house in Stuart for free handouts of freshly caught fish. The fishermen never charged a dime for these gifts, although they could have sold the fish on the market.

The fishermen were an independent bunch, wise in the ways of nature and a few gifted with the art of expression were happy philosophers. Their way of life—like that of the Indians, the Dyaks and the Polynesians—was the only way of life they loved. It was a good life, a strictly masculine life, and an escape and a refuge from the artificialities of civilization.

It was about as elemental as you can get. You drank your water out of an old stone jug that you hoisted up over your shoulder. You lived in an atmosphere of sturdy, useful things: stout oars, sharp knives, strong ropes and seaworthy boats.

The fishermen had the art of relaxation worked out to the nth degree, being able to sleep like babies on the hard floorboards of a boat while waiting for the tide to turn, or to doze away an afternoon on a pile of tarred nets.

Night or day, they responded to the tides and went out on the bays and the sea. They were alive to the meaning of the winds and they saw the stars that so many of us never see.

Those of us who knew them recall the old fish houses with nostalgia; a woman might come to the foot of the dock and yell for her mate, but she didn't dare come out to the dark mysterious fish house, reserved for men only. Her presence there was taboo. Historical interests should preserve at least one old fish house, stock it with nets, cards, jugs, bottles and a sign: "For Men Only."

10

Mean Old Blindey Was Independent; He Kept His Word

Disappearing from the American scene is the mean old bum—and the country is worse without him.

Like old elephants banished from the herd and toothless wolves outlawed by the pack, the old bum was defiantly independent to the end. He was the grizzled rogue of the genus *Homo sapiens,* which he detested.

Before welfare and our sanitized society, the mean old bum was a shining example of the rugged spirit of man versus circumstance. He was the equal of all men and the envy of small boys, whom he tolerated. He was tricky, shifty, dirty, obnoxious and hostile.

I have known many a mean old bum, but the Blind Fisherman was the cream of the crop. He hated women with an unholy hate because some vicious harridan, probably for good reason, had thrown lye on his face. He trusted no one. He had been a catfish trotliner on

Lake Okeechobee and he knew his trade. Back in the Great Depression of the early thirties, this blind old man rowed from the big lake down St. Lucie Canal and set up camp under a canvas fly at Speedy Point just across the St. Lucie River from our town.

I called on him one evening, attracted by the smell of woodsmoke and frying fish. Never will I forget my reception. The two white eyes in his hawklike face with those terrible scars followed my every move. Sightless, he had the hearing of a bat. He allowed me the amenities of introducing myself, and offered me food and coffee—the unwritten law of the river—but he told me without quibble that he had one little rule: "Keep your distance, Mister."

He questioned me closely about the contour of the river's banks downstream, how far he was from the bridges, where docks were with their pilings, and the location of the closest fish house, which was the old Blakeslee fish house across the river down a bit.

Old Blindey spent a week poking around the shorelines in his rowboat. He bumped into bridge pilings, he hit docks—but only once. He established a marvelous map in his mind which amazed all of us who had been watching him with such curiosity, wondering what he was up to.

Soon we found what had brought Old Blindey the long way down from Lake Okeechobee. He was bettering his circumstances. Those were hard times and the price of catfish had hit bottom—anyhow, the average 'Chobee cat weighs only a pound or two and half of that when dressed—but the jewfish in the St. Lucie were bringing four cents a pound whole at Fulton

Market in New York, which meant that the fish house here got two cents and paid one cent a pound.

The blind fisherman was up to catching jewfish, those giant members of the grouper family which come up from the sea into our river to lurk under bridges and docks. He used stout handline made of sash cord and shark hooks baited with live catfish. For him the 50-pounders and the 100-pounders were child's play, but the epics of Old Blindey struggling to bring in a 300 or 400-pounder to the fish house dock live on in our waterfront lore.

His victory against hard times evoked the admiration of all the fishermen. He easily boated the smaller jewfish, but when he hung on to a buster he tied the rope to the stern and let his oars do the work. The sullen giant grouper would pull him backward occasionally, but the old man would bend to the sticks and gain ground. He always won.

On those occasions when he would be towing in a whopper, the seine crew at the fish house would pass the word that "Old Blindey's got him a real money fish," and they would shout encouragement. When the skiff would be pulled backward, they would yell: "Come on Blindey, bring him in!" And, at the final conquest, they would all pitch in, get a rope through Leviathan's gills, and hoist it on a windlass thrashing up into air to be weighed.

The old man always insisted on being paid on the spot. He carried his money in a Prince Albert can in his dirty pants. He would not accept bills. His wants were few and the tobacco can soon became heavy with silver.

One night a young punk—we had them then as now—tried to slip up on him and steal his money. But Old Blindey could hear a fly lighting on a blade of grass. Besides, he had extra-sensory perception and the sharpest knife on the river. Dr. F. B. Eurit took 62 stitches to close the wounds and he remarked at the time that whoever did the carving had a fine sense of how not to kill somebody while teaching him a lesson.

Old Blindey packed all his gear and grub and lines and hooks and tent fly and rowed by the fish house next morning. He cursed everybody in unmentionable depth and announced he was going off to some civilized place to make a living. He rowed down the river into limbo and we were sorry to see him go.

Trying to rob a blind man struck us all as sort of low down. When a deputy sheriff came by to investigate, the fishermen said that the last they saw of Old Blindey he had been rowing *upstream.* The deputy was sort of decent himself and went that way.

We liked Old Blindey. He was mean, dirty and a bum, but a man of his word. When he said "Keep your distance, Mister," he wasn't kidding.

11

The Night That Shorty Joe Was the Hero of the Storm

This is the story of a seine crew that made a rescue in downtown Stuart during the fierce hurricane of 1933.

The hero was a barrel chested fisherman called Shorty Joe. No one knew his last name and everyone was too polite to inquire. He was one of those roustabout drifters common to the time, just before social security numbers had been invented, when a man could be a man without a full name or a number, working on dredges, bridge construction or, in Joe's case, helping to haul in the huge "Black Marias" which encircled the fish of the river.

Shorty Joe was a mighty man on the cork-line, almost as good as the old heaving engine itself that went "Ka-chung! Ka-chung!" as it tugged in the mile long tarred nets to the shoreline in those days before they were outlawed.

69

Shorty Joe was a yard and half tall and about two yards wide when he extended his mighty arms. He looked like he had been hit on the head by a pile driver when real young, with no more injurious effect than to compress him, so that he was just as much of a man as a six-footer, although on the horizontal instead of the vertical.

Shorty was a man among men, not only able to hold his own or better in the occasional rough and tumbles that occurred along the river shore, but it was also said that once he got those mighty arms around the middle of an opponent, the fight was over. He had the grip of a bear and the pugnacity of a bulldog. He took personal pride in being able to perform feats of strength that were too much for others. He was not a team man. He was a show-off. He preferred to do his feats of strength casually, after others had failed, never asking for help and, if anyone commented afterward when he had pulled boats up on the bank or had lifted single handedly a stuck Ford out of the sand, Joe would shrug and say:

"Nothin' to it."

On the evening of the mighty hurricane, after the net boats had all been tied down in the hurricane refuges of distant mangrove creeks, and the fish house doors battened down, those members of the seine crew who did not have any homes to go to—and a few who did—adjourned to the bar in the heart of town.

There they and a few other hardy citizens of the community partook of pain killer, attempting to drown out the rising shriek of the terrible wind, the pounding gusts of torrential rain and the occasional clatter of roofs being torn off and chimneys falling.

When word was brought in that the town's pioneer grocery store had been smashed flat, they had a drink on it. And when someone staggered in to report that the bowling alley had smashed the Woman's Club building like a bug, they had two drinks on that. They had several out of tender recollection when they heard that the old fish house had been blown off its pilings and destroyed along the shore.

But eventually, as occurs in the worst of hurricanes, the bartender turned out the lights and hustled them out into the cruel storm. By that time, they were, indeed, a band of brothers, holding on to each other as the mighty gusts blew them across the railroad tracks, over Flagler Avenue—our Main Street of that era—and into the front door of the Peacock Arcade, a neo-Spanish boomtime structure.

After the hardy fishermen had made it to the refuge of the arcade, more or less involuntarily, Dick Mothershed spoke up. You could always depend on Dick to bring up something unpleasant. "Fellows," he said, "I hate to mention this, but somebody is lying over there in that pile of boards along the track around the express shed. It's a lady," he added, "I heard her squealing and moaning. She's bad hurt."

The wind had risen in intensity. Pieces of sheet-metal roofing were flying through the air, along with Spanish tiles, and the rain was like the blast of a battery of fire hoses. But the fishermen listened and, sure enough, mingled with the furious noises of the storm were pitiful moans and treble falsettos.

Joe was pretty much an anti-social citizen. He did

not hold the respectable townsfolk in too high esteem. "So it's a lady, so what?" he remarked. "Probably one of those who sends the town marshal to break up our poker parties and drunks. Let her alone," said Joe. "You guys couldn't save her if you tried. What business has she got out there causin' trouble on a night like this? Why the hell should we save her? I'm stayin' here."

Three of the strongest and biggest fishermen linked arms, plunged out into the blow, but were blown back in by the winds of the hurricane. It was their defeat that challenged him, not the spark of chivalry.

"Out of my way," said Shorty Joe, "and let a man take over." Fortifying himself from the last of a bottle someone had lifted when the heartless bartender's back was turned, he bent low like a charging bull, his mighty arms swinging, and plunged out into the hurricane.

Ten minutes passed. The storm was at its terrible height. The wind sounded like express trains roaring through town. The rain was like pellets of BBs coursing at 170 miles an hour. It seemed impossible that anyone, even Shorty Joe with his great strength, could effect the rescue.

Dick Mothershed saw them first. "He's got her! He's got her!" he yelled. We all rushed up to the arcade opening to the see the wind rolling the bodies of Shorty Joe and the lady across Flagler Avenue, his mighty arms locked securely around her ample waist.

He didn't let go until he had her safe in the arcade. She didn't have any clothes on. She didn't even say thanks. She was a 250-pound hog that had been blown into town from somewhere out in the country.

I have always thought that Joe deserved the Carnegie
Medal just the same, although he would probably have
shrugged it off with a modest: "Nothin' to it."

12

A Genius Found a Way to Outwit "Hoover Chickens"

Overheard a Floridian the other day offering a boy fifty cents apiece "for all the gopher turtles you can bring me."

Since he was an old friend, I chided him for "getting so lazy you won't dig your own gophers any more" and he owned up to being slothful. "The need just ain't so pressin' as it used to be," he commented. "Remember when we called them 'Hoover Chickens'?"

I did indeed. Back in the closing days of the Hoover administration, the promise of "a chicken in every pot" had fallen through so dismally that anything edible in the countryside was substituted.

In many parts of the South, cottontail rabbits were called "Hoover Chickens" and in our part of South Florida the gopher tortoise, an edible land turtle, was a life-saver for genuinely poverty stricken families long before Welfare or the Poverty War.

The "Hoover Chicken" resided—and still does—in long tunnels slanted back into the spruce terrain of high, dry backwoods sections. The herbivorous tortoises—their favorite food is wire grass—are mostly nocturnal in habit, although occasionally you'll encounter one rocking along on its trail in daylight.

They doubtless feel most secure down at the ends of their 15 to 20-foot long tunnels, six to eight feet under the surface, and they were until hard times spurred hungry men to extra effort. During the Great Depression, the gopher hunter was a common sight in our woods as he prowled with a long, limber hook-pole over his shoulder, carrying a croaker sack and a shovel.

When he found a gopher hole, he would push the pole down the tunnel and fiddle around, sometimes for half an hour, to hook the tortoise by the carapace and haul it out.

The gopher hunter was a single minded man, the sort who never gave up. If a smart tortoise wedged its feet into both sides of the hole at the end of its tunnel and refused to be pulled out, its nemesis would carefully triangulate its position "by guess and by gosh," dig directly down and, with Herculean labor, dig it out.

One such in our community was a leathery old Cracker called Gopher Smith. It was said of him that he had never let one go. He lived in a shack up on the banks of the North Fork, lived richly on gopher stew and cabbage palm hearts, and even had enough to spare to make the rounds in town, offering "Sweet turtle meat, a dime a pound."

But old age got him as it will us all and the old man became too feeble to pursue relentlessly the gopher tribe. Toting a hook-pole wearied him and he didn't have the strength to dig the critters out any more. But Gopher Smith was a genius. He figured a way. He was still able to dig out a hole a couple feet deep in front of a gopher burrow and sink a bean crate or a bushel basket into it. A tortoise in the burrow going out or a gopher turtle returning home was bound to fall in. Kindly, he left a handful of wire grass in the bottom of each basket. If he was delayed a few days in harvesting his crop, the "Hoover Chickens" could munch away at their favorite food.

Once when I was camped up the river, I ran into a deserted field where old Gopher Smith had set out his bean crates in front of half a dozen burrows. It struck me as fiendishly clever, but when I found one poor turtle baking at the bottom of a crate, I broke the unwritten law of the wilderness. I reached down, took it out, patted it on the rump and let it go. One of his.

Old Gopher Smith tore up my camp next day when I was away. He slashed my tent, threw my pots and pans into the scrub palmetto and tossed my grub into the river. I didn't blame him. I deserved it.

His ingenious method of harvesting gophers fortunately never caught on. It would have wiped out the gopher tribe. The Great Depression ended with most Crackers still figuring they had to earn their gophers by the sweat of their brows.

I was tempted for a moment to pass the idea on to the boy who was offered fifty cents apiece for all he could bring in. I was about to say: "Just put you out a bean crate route, Sonny, and you'll have a productive business built up in no time," but thought better of it.

The gophers deserve a fairer shake. They should be worked for, not found, like turtles dropping off a tree.

13

Reflections on Reflections on a Jungle River

Drifting on the surface of a Florida jungle river, like the South Fork of the St. Lucie or the Northwest Branch of the Loxahatchee, I experience the feeling that nothing is ordinary, nothing is commonplace.

The onyx surface of the water reflects in perfect color the images of the bushy headed cabbage palms, the moss draped live-oaks and cypresses along the banks.

Cascading clumps of wild asters and a fragile white spider-lily are mirrored on the the smooth blank film. I drift in my rowboat on top of an image of scenery. There is, probably, a natural law which some logically minded egghead can recite to explain how a color image can be reflected on the face of a river, but please don't quote it. I'd rather marvel.

What has happened to awe? Where has wonder gone? I suspect that too much has been "explained" by the

79

ignorant to the stupid. Modern man's greatest loss of spirit may be that he has ceased to be amazed at the wonders all around him.

Looking up from the tunnel of trees one sees more intimately the blue sky and white clouds. Why blue? Why white? Why are the palm fronds that glittering green? Why is that crimson color on the air plant's flowering spikes? I glance at the molten sun above the palm trees. Just a glance. What frailty is in us that we cannot ever look the sun in the eye? I remember a snatch of Alfred Noyes' poem to the sun: "My light upon the far, faint planets that attend me . . . whose flowers watch me with adoring eyes . . . "

A flower can do what a man cannot; it can look the sun in the eye. Mighty Ra to whom the ancient Egyptians built temples on the banks of Nile. The Sun God who controlled the seasons, the droughts and the floods. We smile at the fantasies of the Pharaohs and have replaced them with a plain, old ordinary sun among millions like it sending out radiation as it burns nuclear fuel. But it still does what Ra did—and sunlight remains as great a mystery now as then.

The river on which I drift begins in that distant, flaming sphere pouring out rays of light that suck mists from the sea to make clouds in the sky.

So simple a process. There's really nothing to it. Just done with light. All of the rivers and all of the clouds all over the world are children of a star. The sun is their father, the sea is their mother and they are born and reborn again so long as the light shines on the waters. We yawn at continuing creation. It is all explainable, if you just have a logical mind. I'm glad I don't.

I would make a good Druid. I believe in magic and in miracles, in mysteries and wonders, and that trees, mountains, rivers, even clouds and certain secret places have personalities. I like storms. I enjoy watching the maneuvering of giant thunderheads, edging around each other, moving in closer, muttering and grumbling and threatening, coming together and destroying each other with furies of winds, crashes of lightning and deluges of rain.

They remind me of the ponderous movements of great governments coming in on each other toward a war which everyone wants to avoid—until caught in the thick of it, when all must make the best of it. One is a storm of mist, the other a storm of belief—and the second is the least tangible and the most destructive. The sun makes one from water; we form the other from thoughts and beliefs. As we believe, they are shaped. What a power for good or evil is the human mind, making its own storms, malignant and benign.

Storms up the river remind me of creatures that sneak up and pounce. You hear them muttering, you see them coming, you figure they are going to miss you—and there is a time when you could do something about avoiding them. Then there is a point of no return. You are definitely caught, can do nothing to escape. There is no place to go.

You look at the bright side. You are glad you are not in a small boat at sea. You are going to get wet, but you are not going to be drowned. You are, after all, a land creature, and having shielding trees and firm land close by is relatively comforting. How human it is that our first thought about the threat of nuclear storms is that perhaps—just perhaps, but hopefully—we may burrow into the earth and escape.

Hauled under a leaning palm, I endure the storm, but it finds me out and soaks me to the skin. And it is gone. Nothing is so completely gone as a storm that has passed or Druids or Pharaohs or empires in which people have stopped believing.

There are trickles and rivulets and creeklets coming into the river, making it whole again, flowing to the sea to be warmed once more by the sun and made into clouds to fill the river again.

What is light? I glance at incandescent Ra, but dare not look him in the eye. "You wet me good," I say. "Now warm me up."

14

An Afternoon in a Quiet Place Far Up the River

Moonshiners and outlaws like quiet places—and so do I. If Lady Bird Johnson would just ask my help in her campaign to beautify the nation, I have a tip: "Save the quiet places first. Make national shrines of every moonshine still site in America."

This would save a lot of effort by committees that don't know one piece of scenery from another. The moonshiner has something to give to his country—aesthetic taste and discrimination on the beauties of nature. He is a connoisseur at combining the artful camouflage of shrubbery and trees with pure spring water in hidey-holes where nobody can see him but he can see in all directions.

We sorely need places like that to revive the souls and refresh the spirits of harried Americans. I have a list of about 25 such beauty spots in Martin County, only five of them currently operating. Last Saturday

afternoon I revisited The Little Gem.

The Little Gem is far, far up the river, so artfully concealed that it was only by the oddest happenstance many years ago that I found it. Going upriver, I noticed that a Cracker friend of mine was cane pole fishing from a rowboat close to the bank on a jungle reach. But, most oddly, he and the rowboat had disappeared when I came downriver half an hour later.

I scrounged along the bank, just fishing, of course, until I found where overhanging mangrove limbs screened off a winding tunnel waterway not more than five feet wide. As I lifted a limb to get a better view, a swarm of wasps stung my face and hands. Fair enough. All quiet places should have guarded portals. And they are not to be visited while devoted to industrial use.

A year or two later, when I noticed that my Cracker friend was cane pole fishing on another stretch of river, I slipped my rowboat into the tunnel and, smarting from wasp stings, I poled to the quiet place. I had to pull the boat over fallen palm trees. I got redbugs. Those horrible crab-spiders kept falling on my face. But The Little Gem was worth it.

The tunnel wound for 1,000 yards and opened into a beautiful pool, fed by a bubbling spring, with blue sky and white clouds above. Towering cabbage palms and venerable live-oaks, draped with Spanish moss and orchids, rimmed the banks. A flock of white egrets rose as I drifted out on the still water. It was, and is, a perfect place. A couple of weathered oaken barrels, their staves askew, added to the atmosphere.

Last Saturday it was unchanged. There are houses with swimming pools now up and down the river and a

snazzy Country Club with two golf courses within deer
rifle distance of The Little Gem. You'd never know it. I
drifted in timeless peace, watching a cloud of midges
dance, each to itself a self.

Once more I enjoyed a trick of sitting motionless,
being absolutely quiet, which is the lost art of
disappearing. A striped-necked turtle stuck up its head
and watched me suspiciously with beady eyes for 15
minutes. A pileated woodpecker hammered away on a
palm bole and two grey squirrels had a race, leaping
from frond to frond. Gars rolled and bluegills struck at
fallen insects. I watched a water spider skate across the
surface. A chameleon fell from a branch and just made
it ashore one skittering jump ahead of a hungry bass. In
the quiet of the evening the egrets came in to roost and
I missed Old One Eye.

Fourteen feet long if he was an inch, he used to be
the lord of that place, with his knobby right eye that
had seen so much—the left one had been shot out—and
his serrated tail all chewed up in battles. He used to lay
for calves up by Cane Creek before they dredged it.
Somebody finished him off about fifteen years ago. He
is a legend now. I think they named the Greater 'Gator
stores for him.

I saw Old One Eye on the river a number of times
but at The Little Gem just once—he saw me first. He
hit the pool from the bank like seventeen barrels of
concrete launched by a catapult—and it scared me to
think that anything that big was scared of me. Anyhow,
The Little Gem's still there.

As the panther changes its lair, the 'shiner switches
from beauty spot to beauty spot. Assuming that there

are half a million pristine still sites in the country—probably a low estimate—400,000 are surplus. That is a lot of beauty. If made available, there should be a gentleman's agreement not to use those where "Do Not Disturb" placards are posted unobtrusively. Fair is fair.

Quiet places, when not serving industrial needs, should be enjoyed. They are America's pre-selected shrines. If Lady Bird agrees, I'll try to get my Cracker friend to give us the secret of how he gets the wasp nests started and keeps them going. Quiet places aren't any good without wasp nests at their gates.

15
Jungle Rivers, Places of Beauty and of Peace

The upper waters of the jungle rivers of Florida's East Coast—the Loxahatchee and the North Fork and South Fork of the St. Lucie—loop like serpents under the sun.

On the shores of the broad estuaries and bays of their lower reaches are small towns growing into cities and waterfront subdivisions march upstream. But, as yet, the little rivers of the headwaters are untouched.

They are bordered by dense and luxuriant growth suggesting that the boatman is exploring serpentine black branchlets of the Amazon or the Orinoco but, in fact, the high sand lands of pine and scrub palmetto are never more than a few hundred feet away. They give the illusion that they are far from civilization. They are not, which is sad, because they would last longer if they were truly remote and inaccessible.

The Northwest Branch of the Loxahatchee coming

up from Jupiter is dark, brooding, mysterious–and amazingly beautiful. Cypresses give this stream its greatest charm. There are patriarchs eighty feet tall and five feet thick, here when Columbus landed on San Salvador, living giants draped in beards of grey Spanish moss. Along the palm-bordered banks are cascades of wild asters in full bloom, delicate white spider-lilies and that carnivorous tree, the strangler fig, swallowing other trees like an anaconda swallowing its prey. What a cunning, contriving, deadly species!

The mature strangling fig is like a Bluebeard turned respectable burgher. It is a fat boled, umbrella shaped, graceful tree with glistening green leaves and attractive red berries which resemble tiny figs. Birds love the berries and one of a hundred thousand of the seeds that they pass lodges in the crevice of a cabbage palm or a gumbo-limbo limb, sprouts high in the air, sends down a tiny, swaying tendril. The tendril enters the ground and becomes a stout root wrapped around the host tree. More tendrils drop and more roots encase the host, merging with one another, encasing the victim, squeezing it to death.

There is drama in the upper rivers.

The Loxahatchee has heard the hiss of the advancing subdivisions but a large portion of it has been saved by inclusion in Jonathan Dickinson State Park and by acquisition of a stretch as an Audubon Society sanctuary. The river is still under the threat of siltation from citrus grove drainage canals to the west.

The South Fork and North Fork of the St. Lucie upstream from Stuart are not so fortunate. They still exist on the edge of the sword of private ownership.

The owners must pay taxes and sooner or later they must either develop or sell to developers.

These are lovely and beautiful places which should be preserved forever as they are for future generations to enjoy. Their jungle scenery of cabbage palms, live-oaks and water maples, bordered by lush giant ferns, spider-lilies and custard apples, enveloped by wild asters, moon vines and fox grapes, is so dense that it takes the stiffest breeze to ripple the waters. Most of the time, the surface is mirror-smooth, black as polished onyx, perfectly reflecting the beauty of the trees with their crimson spiked air plants, shoestring ferns and delicate wild orchids.

They are the haunts of black bass and bluegills, gars, mudfish and leather shelled turtles. Tarpon roll in the dark waters and the placid manatee seeks their quiet to bear and nurse its young.

They are precious places wrapped in a magic spell which can not endure the encroachment of housing or development. The moment a house appears on one of these banks, the illusion of being far away and deep in a jungle will be broken.

It took hundreds of thousands of years to create the perfect scenery of our jungle rivers, but they are so vulnerable that one bulldozer and an efficent construction crew could destroy what is there in a few weeks. What remained might still seem beautiful, with lawns and landscaping and people, but the unique wild beauty nature made would be forever gone.

If this were truly an enlightened state, Florida would find a means to purchase these unspoiled upper rivers and put them in the public trust to be enjoyed forever.

They are among the few places left where you can still find the harried alligator baking in the sun on the bank, not yet a victim of the hide hunter. Here you can still see egrets and ibises silhouetted against the sunset as they fly to their rookeries.

The upper rivers are unique. There is nothing else like them in America. When they are gone, there will be no more.

A marvelous experience open to each and every one of us here now is to enjoy the blessed peace and beauty of the unspoiled upper rivers.

They are sanctuaries for observation and contemplation. On them you will see the water turkey, also called anhinga and snake bird, a relict of those days when reptiles learned to fly. Still more at home in the water than in the air, it swims submerged, with a few inches of neck and head protruding in pulsing forward-backward movement. When it takes to flight, it is a gawky, clumsy, awkward creature, reminding one of the great effort which it must have taken for the first birds to learn to fly.

On these little rivers you can still see otters playing and the lordly diamondback rattlesnake, a very king of dignity and death, swimming across majestically, head erect, his precious rattles kept up out of the water.

There are pileated woodpeckers, often mistaken for the nearly extinct ivory-bill, and happy mullet leaping just for the fun of it. Giant black and yellow spiders with jeweled eyes spin their webs and graceful yellow and black tiger swallowtail butterflies end their short sweet lives by blundering into them.

I love the upper rivers. When I was a boy, I used to camp on them, sitting in the dark listening to the low, thrumming roar of bull alligators or hearing palm fronds crackle as raccoons circled the camp. One night a leopard frog hopped up to the embers of my fire to warm itself. I sort of felt I knew him and next day, when I heard the pitiful cry of a frog caught in the jaws of a snake, I took the trouble to release it. Sort of didn't know the snake.

May all the fish I have jerked out of those waters on a cane pole when they hit an imitation pork rind frog forgive me.

I find peace in the upper rivers. Their charm is that you can still be alone on them, look up to the stars or the clouds and think. They unlock the mind and its friend, the spirit.

Their waters remind me of the Psalms and their beauty of what the hand of God has done.

Why, I wonder, do we spend billions of dollars to get to the cold, bleak, barren, inhospitable landscape of the moon, but can not afford to save for our children's children a veritable Eden close at hand?

Inevitably, these magic quiet places will be gone, the beauty of the jungle destroyed by what we call progress: houses, beer cans, water skiers and TV antennae.

They will be used, as every other place of beauty is, for waterfront homes, country clubs, yacht basins and marinas—but when human beings roost on them their true charm will vanish. No finer use could be found for the upper rivers than to leave them as they are.

We build churches of wood and stone but fail to preserve the living cathedrals of nature, which can never be rebuilt with human hands.

16

The Mysterious Mangroves
Are Secret Places

The red mangrove tree, standing on stilts, looking like a crouching creature, is tropically artistic, although it is usually the first victim of bulldozing when a piece of riverfront land is cleared.

There seems to be an inherent antagonism on the part of mankind against the mangroves. Giant dredges suck sand from the bays to fill, kill and smother ecological wonders so men can have more high-rise condominiums. It is a needless destruction of Florida beauty when decorative shoreline mangroves are cut down to be replaced by stark concrete sea walls.

Perhaps only naturalists admire the mangrove trees. They seem to me to have almost animal-like spirit and intelligence. Much of our coastal land has been built by these aggressive trees, edging out into the shallows, sending down tapered roots from above to pierce the mud tenaciously. They tiptoe forward, grimly hold each bit of gained ground.

They are born as white flowers from which grow foot long, tapering seeds—like long, thin, pointed greenish-brown cigars. The seeds fall into the water and float, pointed end down, for miles upon miles on the tides and currents. Millions of them are cast above the high tide line by the waves, where they shrivel and die, but a fortunate few bob into quiet little coves and shoreline eddies where their pointed tips take root.

Some go far up the North and South Forks of the St. Lucie, as far as there is a trace of salinity which they must have. When you have passed the last little mangrove bush among the cabbage palms and live-oaks that border the upper streams, it is a sign that you have at last reached pure fresh water.

Occasionally, on our lower bays, you see a lonely little mangrove on a point of land, sort of an advance guard, stubbornly holding the soil which it has gained, resisting wind and waves, a defiant little tree needing only time and good fortune to make its foothold secure.

But it is in the great swamps themselves, where the victory has been won, that you sense the real spirit of the mangroves. Their organization is a complex society. The red mangroves—the squatty, spider-like trees on whose roots the 'coon oysters grow—are the warriors in the forefront, the land gainers, standing against storm with their buttressed roots, fringing all the waters and twisting, tunnel-like creeks.

Behind them are white mangroves, tall, pole-like trees, growing close together in soldierly ranks. And standing like patriarchs of the jungle are the black mangroves which are like forest oaks except for their tiny leaves. They are gnarled and massive and their wood is harder than mahogany. Some of them were here before Ponce de Leon landed in Florida. Sawed sections of two black mangrove trees taken from the great swamp at the south end of Hutchinson Island were given a growth ring count at the University of Florida. One proved to be more than 400 years old, the other more than 500.

The spirit of a mangrove swamp, well established, centuries old, is one of complacent victory. It has seized land from the shallows and held it through the hurricanes of centuries.

Today, when the footsteps of men are just about everywhere, and their airboats zoom across the wildest saw grass Everglades, a big mangrove swamp is one of the few places left that offers seclusion and privacy. They afford refuges for the rookeries of wading birds, and for the nests of eagles and ospreys.

Yet, despite their forbidding borders, the big swamps are far from impenetrable. Little winding creeks go far into their hearts. If you don't mind getting your feet wet, you can climb through the roots and overhanging limbs of the warrior trees at the borders and come into comparatively open ground in the interior.

You will find a few scattered, peaceful and quiet cabbage palm islands in the heart of a great mangrove swamp. There are occasional oyster shell kitchen middens of the vanished Carib tribes which once lived along Florida's coasts. The palm islands are open and airy, with hardly any underbrush, and the sun streams down into them. They are the haunt of the diamondback rattlesnake and the brown marsh rabbit on which it feeds. They are crossed by the trails of raccoons and wildcats and every palm tree bears the criss-cross scratches of hundreds of creatures which have climbed them to feed on the clusters of pungent black berries high above.

These islands are refuges for one of the most interesting of all crabs, the tree climbing land hermit, a vigorously aggressive, pink, violet and red creature inhabiting abandoned moon shells. The land hermit, unlike most water hermits which are timid and self effacing, stands little nonsense from man. If you pick him up by the shell that is his home, he will stand the indignity a few seconds, then come rustling out to nip at your fingers. There are also beautiful tree snails on the mangrove trees. Occasionally you find nursery pools swarming with baby tarpon, snook and other fish, waiting to be liberated on a high spring tide.

Big mangrove swamps are living museums of the pioneer past. In them you will find old crockery jugs and ancient bottles washed over the rim of the dunes fifty or a hundred years ago.

The big swamps fall only to devastating super-hurricanes, erosion by the sea or man's bulldozers and sand pumping dredges.

It is sad to see them go. We can destroy but never replace what took five centuries to grow.

17

Cabbage Palms Are Florida's Most Marvelous Trees

Back in the 1920's I camped a spell with Jesse Baker in a hammock on the old Steamboat Passage near Peck's Lake.

Jesse was a real outdoorsman. He was the best man to cut a cabbage I ever saw. With a sharp axe, he would take three or four horizontal strokes at just the proper height on the tree where the sweet palm heart ended and the bitter began, then cross the inverted T with four or five vertical strokes, reach in and pull out the cabbage.

Sounds easy. Looks easy, too, when done by an expert—but it is an exhausting job of work for the greenhorn. First, you must find a fat young tree, with solid boots on its outside, and then you must know by looking at it just how far down below those boots the heart extends. If you cut too high, you'll split the heart—and if you cut too low you'll be rewarded with pithy wood.

Jesse's hearts of palms were always perfect, flawlessly white, pristinely clean, so crisp and nutty in flavor that you couldn't resist eating a few slices raw as you shredded them cross-wise with a sharp knife for the pot.

Of course, we're getting so civilized now that somebody owns everything and I wouldn't be surprised if cutting a cabbage is a crime, but back then we ate the trees for vegetables without giving a hoot whose land they were on—and how delicious they were!

There were two schools of cabbage palm cookery. Either one turned out a product fit for the gods. Most frontier woodsmen preferred to simmer a few dozen diced cubes of salt pork in the bottom of a cast-iron dutch oven, dump in the sliced palm cabbage and semi-fry it, then throw in a cup of water and slow steam it with the lid on tight. Another method was to add a lot more water, shake in a little evaporated milk and a few sliced onions, allowing the pot to simmer for an hour or two. A few regarded addition of the onions and canned milk as heresy.

No early-day Floridian ever felt the slightest worry about not having enough to eat. Wherever he looked, there were hammocks of cabbage palms with their hearts free for the taking, rivers and bays full of fish and woods filled with game.

The cabbage palm—only a botanist or a landscape artist calls it the sabal—is Florida's most wonderful tree. You can eat it, sleep on its leaves, and they will snugly thatch a lean-to or shack.

We used to make our "woods mattresses" with a

foundation of cabbage palm fronds laid fish scale fashion, on top of which we would place three or four layers of the smaller palmetto fans. It was sort of rough the first couple of nights, but after the springiness wore down the combination made about as fine a sleeping arrangement as you could expect on the ground.

For a permanent camp, it was little trouble to make a lean-to or chickee, threading the palm fronds between thin pine saplings. We used to trim down a long, straight palm branch, cut a wide needle eye in one end to hold a rag, and make a perfect shotgun cleaning rod. The trapper used trimmed green palm limbs to square-stretch 'coon hides. The trick was to cut slits along the edges of a green hide, thread four palm sticks in the slits, on sides, top and bottom, pull the sticks tightly away from each other and tie the corners.

We used the boots or dry butts of the palm fronds, which protect the young tree from the elements but fall as it starts to grow tall, and also the dried limbs, to make a smokeless cooking fire.

If mosquitoes bothered—as they frequently did—the palm tree again was your friend. You took the compressed leaves in the top of the heart, shredded them so they resembled a horse's tail and flailed away at the pesky skeeters with it. An expert could walk through a swamp with a palm mosquito switch, slapping his face, hands and knees with such rhythmic precision that only a few of the thousands of mosquitoes flying in on him would reach target.

Wives of the early settlers were experts at weaving wide brimmed hats from split fibers taken from the top of the cabbage palm heart.

Rafts of cabbage palm logs used to be drifted down the rivers to form the piling of Florida docks.

Blessed cabbage palms! How many times I have had a fine meal from you, slept on your leaves, eaten your pungent black berries, cooked camp meals on fires from your dried limbs and served them on plates made from your shiny green leaves.

No other tree has ever been so generous. But never climb one of the tall giants that has shed its boots and towers high in the hammock. I did so once on the old sand ridge which rimmed wild Lake Okeechobee before Conner's Highway was built. It was easy going up but, on the way down, I found that every sharp fiber of the outside bark points upward, and came down with my arms and chest loaded with splinters.

The cabbage palm's revenge was a small price to pay for knowing it better. I had liked it before; after that I also respected it.

18

Spruce Woods on Old Dunes Full of Life

The little "Florida spruce," a type of dwarfed white pine, chooses our dry, sandy dunes for its habitat. The trees in every wood lean in the direction of the dominant wind of their lifetime. You'll see them on the sand hills west of Jensen Beach, on rolling sand knolls in the eastern part of Jonathan Dickinson State Park, and scattered on high ridges near Gomez, west of Stuart, on upper Bessey Creek and at Spruce Bluff on the North Fork.

Their chosen living space is the white "sugar sand" of dunes that bordered ancient seas. It is the most arid, least fertile, highest and driest soil of our region. Thousands of acres of spruce pine land in our part of Florida, from Fort Pierce to Stuart and on down Sewall's Point, were cleared and planted to Cuban Red or Spanish pineapples from the 1880's to 1915. The pineapple, a bromeliad, thrived on the arid soil—and

when the plantations failed, the little spruce pines took
the land back, as if foreclosing a mortgage.

Flora of the spruce region includes dwarf hickories
and scrub oaks, planted there by the frisky Florida grey
squirrels, which love to nibble the mast and cones of
the spruce and to nest in its boughs. There are clinging
orange-yellow "love vines" and puffy grey-green lichens
on the ground that architects use as "miniature trees"
to landscape down-scaled models.

At first sight, the spruce woods seem lifeless, mostly
because in the heat of the day they are intensely hot.
Your eyes blink at the white glare of the sun reflected
on the shimmering sand. It is ten degrees hotter here
than in the yellow pines and palmettos nearby. You
sweat and wonder why you came.

But then you see a blue tailed skink, loving the heat,
coming up on a rotted log to stick out its forked
tongue again and again. Your eye catches a flash of
checkered red and it is the pulsing throat badge of a
green chameleon issuing its challenge on a palmetto
fan. The spruce is full of life.

You hear a bouncing in the branches and a grey
squirrel comes down to the ground, his pouches full.
You watch it bury a couple of hickory nuts for winter
reserve, and suddenly you know why, when a forest fire
rages through the spruce, it is always followed first by a
new forest of Florida dwarf hickory trees.

An inhabitant which you will never see in the
daytime—your only chance would be to sit still on a
moonlit night—is the nocturnal flying squirrel. These
tiny, big eyed creatures, which have pendulous skin
stretching out like a parachute between rear limbs when

they sail from tree to tree, are much more abundant than is generally known. Their tiny nests are lined with the softest down taken from the furry brown moss found near the base of cabbage palm fronds, and they sleep in them all day long.

At night they are grey shadows slipping from tree to tree on magical veils of air. They sail like flying fishes through the spruce.

Several times I have encountered one of the most interesting of woods families in the spruce, a lady skunk and her young, turning over rotted limbs and rooting for ground insects. A spruce ridge in the wilder part of our county is still apt to be a wild turkey feeding ground early in the morning. The little grey Florida foxes and wildcats also make regular hunting inspections of the spruce woods, leaving their tell-tale tracks behind in the white sand. Opossums and 'coons do not favor the spruce, nor do otter, preferring the ponds, cabbage hammocks, pine woods or mangrove swamps.

In the spruce you will find the greatest concentration of gophers, the Florida dry land tortoises. I suspect that they choose those arid regions because they are so well drained and they can excavate their long, slanted burrows deeply without encountering the danger of underground water.

The high spruce ridges are also the favored home of the huge Florida diamondback rattlesnakes, which have formed a live-and-let-live liaison with the gopher tortoises and take their long, digestive sleeps down at the bottom of the gopher holes, side by side with the tortoises.

The gopher tortoises, which are miniatures of the

great land tortoises of the Galapagos, are placid creatures. They leave their holes to get to the pinelands, where they rock along through trails in the wire grass on their stubby, elephant-like legs, swaying from side to side. They walk with the the deliberate roll of tiny elephants carrying howdahs on their backs and at long periods they stand and ruminate. They are vegetarians, feeding only on grass. As they digest the stuff, they leave oval pellets of compacted grass fibers behind them like so many little bales of hay.

When the diamondbacks leave their underground sleeps in the spruce, they too go prowling off to the flatlands. A Florida rattler, going somewhere, not seeing you, is a majestic sight. He holds his deadly triangular head erect several inches off the ground and seems to flow in a straight line, knowing where he is going, driven by a purpose.

That purpose is either hunger or love—the main motives that impel us all. Food usually comes first. The rattler finds a well defined, fresh used trail of a swamp rabbit, cottontail or woods rat, and coils off to one side of it—the death that waits by the side of the trail.

It will lie there like a taut spring patiently for a day or a night until a warm blooded creature starts to pass. Scientists say that the pits on the top of the rattler's head are sensory organs alerting it to heat and guiding the sinking of its fangs unerringly into warm flesh. This is a system we imitate in our plane-to-plane missiles that seek the hot jets of enemy planes.

The tortoise loaded with grass and the rattlesnake, sluggishly dragging home a whole swamp rabbit inside, alike return to the gopher hole where, like the lion and lamb of biblical prophecy, they lie down together and sleep it off. It is a strange truce in the spruce.

19

The White Birds Hold Jubilee in Drying Ponds

Drought is jubilee time for the white birds in South Florida's marshes. They gather by the thousands in countless drying ponds, potholes and swales, feasting on the trapped and dying creatures of the diminishing waters.

The white birds act as clean-up squads. There are flocks of white wood ibises with naked black heads and black tipped wings. These native American storks trample the bottom and muddy the shallows, scooping up oxygen starved fish that come gasping to the surface.

There are stately white herons and graceful egrets, a few grey herons and little blues, all busily engaged in spearing helpless prey. From pond to pond they go and from swale to swale, cleaning out a place at a time in concerted community action.

Drought brings great days for the white birds, times

113

of transient abundance, and their clamor as they gulp down the denizens of the dying ponds is one of rejoicing, with the spectre of famine on its way. Many of these birds that throng the dying ponds are refugees from Everglades National Park, where the former watery wastes lie sun baked and desolate in drought times. They are like the throngs that flee a famine into cities where there is still food.

Mismanagement of Florida's water resources periodically dries up the Everglades. Lake Okeechobee used to overflow to the southward down through a vast sea of saw grass and shallows, creating a haven for bird and animal life. But the U.S. Engineer Corps put levees around the giant lake, dug canals to the Gulf of Mexico and the Atlantic, to waste billions of gallons of fresh water in the sea.

Now there are fires in the saw grass and the acrid smoke tells of peat being burned down to the bare rock. The Everglades, unique and irreplaceable, are being destroyed. The hot sun shines red through the smoke of a land that is burning to death.

One by one, score by score, even the ponds dry up and the white birds abandon them, going on to the next and the next. Raccoons, 'possums and wildcats come down in the night to feast on stranded bass and bream too big for the birds.

Then, at last, there is no water left at all and the buzzards and carrion crows come down to clean up sun baked gars and mudfish. The white sand of what once were clear shallows glares in the sun and the mud bottomed pond middles stink, wrinkle and crack. There are trails leading from the dried ponds where leather-back turtles have taken to the woods, searching for a residue of water—somewhere.

The alligator holes, last refuge of a few "seed fish" should the rains come again, and they will, are left exposed to the law breaking alligator hunter with his prod hook. He hauls the 'gator out, kills it and skins out its belly hide, writing a final chapter in the death of a pond.

As the drought continues, there are eventually hundreds, thousands of sun baked white circles, blankly blind where the living blue eyes of the ponds once looked to the sky.

The transient jubilee of the white birds is an indictment of men for lowering water tables and wasting South Florida's fresh water. The peninsula has been drained and drained for thirty years; only now are we getting a glimmering of insight that we must store, preserve and hold our fresh waters. They are not forever expendable.

The fish of the ponds do not get a second chance but we will, inevitably, as the hurricanes come, sending down their deluges of rain. Water will fall, as it always has, by the hundreds of billions of gallons, refilling the ponds and the marshes, filling canals and ditches and rushing out to sea.

Not next year or the next, or for many years to come will we learn the lesson that you cannot throw away the water which must soak down into the land and refill the underground aquifers.

But eventually, when we are searching for fresh water as the white birds hunt the last remaining fish in a drought, it may dawn on us that we must save our marshes for natural reservoirs, that somehow we must block and hold back the water, give it time to build up the storage basins under the ground.

We waste enough water in Florida to make the desert bloom—but if we keep on doing it, this can be desert, too.

The ponds drop quickly, your lawn dries out, the garden withers because the underground water tables have been lowered by excessive drainage.

And it will not be "jubilee time" for us if those tables go much lower and the ocean's salt intrudes into the fresh water we all take for granted now.

20

Sandhill Cranes Aren't Whoopers But They Whoop

We get numerous reports at the newspaper office about "whooping cranes" and are urged to send a cameraman with long-range telephoto lens to various parts of the county where the "whoopers" are reported strolling in pastures, feeding and whooping.

They whoop, all right, but they are not whooping cranes. They are sandhills, a tall, grey-brown bird with a red top-knot, varying in color with sex and maturity. Noble and impressive birds, they reach five feet, about a foot shorter than the real whooping crane, largest bird on the American continent, standing as tall as a man.

The real whooper is white with black wing tips. At this writing, there are only about forty of them in existence. They are strongly protected on the Aransas Refuge in southeast Texas, risk their lives in long flights across the nation to raise their young in the Canadian wilderness, and fly south again—running the gantlet

119

both ways of the ignorant and cruel who will shoot at anything that moves.

The sandhill cranes of Florida are a non-migratory population. Under wise conservation education and rigid state and federal protection, they have been increasing. There are several thousand now in the flatwoods of South Florida and, occasionally, they stroll through the remoter subdivisions.

Their cacophonic "aaa-oo-ee, aaa-ooo-eee" is a melodious accompaniment of early morning in our woods. Their cry is most often uttered when they are alarmed and take to flight.

You can pass a flock in an automobile at fairly close range—most birds and some animals seem to have little fear of cars—but a man on foot aiming a camera or even pointing a finger at them is enough to send them winging off.

For good sandhill crane pictures, you must be hidden in a well designed blind and be prepared to sit there for a few hours.

You'll usually find sandhills in flocks of three, five or seven. You'll win two out of three times if you'll bet that the flock consists of an odd number of birds.

They pair off in the spring and perform an elaborate courtship dance, walking forward, bowing, walking back, while they chitter their bills and alternately lower and arch their necks. The dance of the cranes is an elaborate ritual.

The nests are built of sticks and grass elevated above the ground level of the marsh, usually containing from three to five eggs.

Cranes radically differ from herons in that they are

birds of the land, rather than the waters. The herons and egrets—with the exception of the cattle egret, which is mostly an insect eater—wood ibises and all other wading birds live mostly on fish and crawfish.

But the majestic sandhill crane is a seed eater and insect harvester. It patrols recently burned over woodlands and new pastures.

The pioneers used to shoot them and roast them like turkeys, prizing the white flesh of their breasts. Now, thankfully, the sandhills are part of the rich treasury of bird life with which we are blessed in modern Florida. Long may their kind increase. Please warn your children that it is a violation of state and federal law to shoot at them.

21

The Squidder Was the Aristocrat of Fishermen

The squidder was the aristocrat of commercial fishermen along the Florida coast. Like the osprey, he was a machine designed for catching fish selectively and he looked down on all his brethren in the trade.

That included the seiners, who operated huge haul nets in the bays, the drift-netters, stab-netters and hand-liners. He felt himself to be far above the cane-pole poppers, the pigfishermen and the live-mullet-for-bait men. With all those he shared just one thing, a detestation for sport fishermen.

The squidder was strictly an "outside man" and "outside" is the sea. A possible reason for his arrogance, smugness and contempt of those he considered lesser fishermen was that the sea was his constant antagonist. His eyes had that look into the distance of the aviator who puts his life on the line every time he goes up into turbulence.

123

The squidder's time to make money was November through March, when Northern ports were out of business and the fine "hotel fish"—bluefish, Spanish and king mackerel—brought the highest prices at Fulton Market in New York.

That is also the time of the "winter season" when—despite the Chamber of Commerce folders—sporadic "blue northers" and northeasters come romping down into Florida ahead of what are called "unseasonable cold snaps."

There are warm days and cold days, calm days and stormy days, and to all these the reef at St. Lucie Inlet where the squidders went to sea responds in kind.

It was smooth and still until the winds blew and the ground-swells came rolling in to break upon the back of the dragon of coral rock that is the reef. And then that dragon muttered and growled and dared the squidders to come downriver and try to go outside.

The mutter of the dragon was a challenge to the squidders, especially when the blues, the mackerel and the kings were packed up outside in vast migrating schools. They would gather at dawn in their able Jersey-type sea skiffs, engines idling, facing into the threat of the rows of breakers that came thundering into the mouth of the river.

Crest following crest, the breakers moved in majesty, with the wind whipping spume from their tops, and in the hollows of the largest ones the jagged rocky back of the dragon would occasionally show, ready to smash a boat's bottom and break the bones of fishermen.

An angry reef gave the squidder his greatest hour. It was what made him the aristocrat, the man apart from his kind. He waited and he watched for the lull of the flooding tide, he counted the breakers for that seventh wave which is usually a little brother to the rest. He gunned his engine, quartered the breakers, sent spray flying in vast sheets, dodged this way and that way, running the gantlet of crests and hollows, past the last breaker to the victory of "outside."

There his tarred trolling lines went out, two from mangrove outrigger poles, two from the stern, all baited with the bright tin squids which gave him his name. Sleigh bells were attached to the boat ends of the lines and soon they began to jingle merrily as the fish struck. There have never been happier men on the face of this earth than squidders pulling fish when the bells were ringing, hoisting them in the air and down on the de-hooker on the lip of a barrel.

Jingle! Pull! Hoist, unhook and throw the squid back! A squidder in the fish would set his stern tiller for a circle, going around and around the school, jumping like a monkey from line to line, shortening lines, finally handling only two as the barrels filled up. Pull, hoist, unhook and throw that squid back!

Every squidder watched every other squidder as sea gulls watch sea gulls. A squidder's dream was to have the fish all to himself, but that rarely lasted long. The repeated silver flash of hoisted fish on the horizon brought other squid boats and soon the finder of the school was one of a dozen circling the striking fish.

The squidders never cut each other's lines. They went with the established circle, never against it, never across it. They did not like each other much, but they kept the rules.

The closest they came to a fraternity was their huddle to get outside and a huddle again to come in over the dragon of the reef, when the trick was to get on top of the back side of a breaker and ride it in. To fall off the wave was to be broached and capsized by the following sea.

When they unloaded their catches, the fish house man would ask: "How was it outside today?" A proper squidder would reply: "Not bad." Then he would add: "But a little rough getting out and back in."

22

Free Roaming Frontier of the Sea Is Close at Hand

Florida used to be called "the last frontier." Now that roads, agriculture, industry and developments have claimed the land, its people have discovered that the sea so close at hand is the last real frontier.

Abounding with wildlife, as yet undamaged by man, without a barbed wire fence or a "No Trespass!" sign, Florida's ocean edges are today's challenge to adventure. The sea, with its rolling porpoises and giant mantas, sailfish and marlin, sharks and migratory fish more abundant than the passenger pigeons used to be, is the last place where wild creatures are even more plentiful than they once were on the land.

The sea, despite the fences and condominiums, turnpikes and urban sprawl, is available to everyone, uncontrolled, untamed and free, outside all concepts of private ownership, barter, sale, surveys and restrictions which have hemmed in the land. At sea, and only at sea, men still have freedom of movement. There is no road which you must follow. Your course to any point of the compass is determined only by your own decision, tempered by whatever good sense you may have about wind, waves, reefs and breakers.

The freedom of the sea and its abundance of life are lures which draw me out over the St. Lucie reef at sunrise. The clean new day, the fresh sea air, the promise of adventure beckoning, take me and my small outboard powered boat on what is really a combination of "looking-seeing-doing." My boat is a fourteen-footer, small to be at sea, but it is stoutly made and rides the waves like a gull. There is a small spare engine, rarely used, mounted on its stern, two gallon jugs of fresh water up in the bow, 300 feet of spare anchor rope, a package of flares, and a piece of canvas which could be jury-rigged with the oars to sail home.

Sea birds dip and dive and there are spurts of white spray over the shallow flats south of the inlet. I investigate and find Spanish mackerel, bluefish or blue runners striking schools of glass minnows. A few passes with trolled spoons produce enough "eating fish" to supply the family's larder for a week.

A big gold and silver "dinner plate" pompano is frightened by my engine and goes skittering across the surface like a skipped round stone. I stop and drift, jig a little lead and nylon feather on a light spinning rod, add a "gourmet fish" to the ice chest.

Next I head alongshore to the southward, down toward the Land of the Drowned Trees where erosion is eating into the wild coast. There, where the ancient Carib Indians had their towns and left vast shell middens, the sea is gnawing away at the land. Huge black mangroves are being swallowed by the ocean and groves of cabbage palms seem to be marching like lemmings into the sea.

This is the favored spot along our coast for the massing of pilchards, mullet and other bait fish. When they are there, schools of tarpon, king mackerel and sharks can be found charging into them.

The sea is cruel. I note a fleeing sennet, a small, barracuda-like fish, leaping for its life, the last leap ending in a smother of foam where a king mackerel had breakfast.

Passing over the great coral reef on a smooth day, I shut off the motor and drift, looking down at grouper, mangrove snapper, yellow and black porkfish and exotic angelfish threading their way between purple sea plumes. A giant loggerhead turtle comes up for air and sighs. Schools of tiny little balao or half-beaks take to the air and skim on the surface of the sea, their pencil-thin silver bodies slanted in air, their tails wildly thrumming in the water fleeing some nameless dread.

On calm days, I head out over the reef for the Gulf Stream, that magical ribbon of indigo-blue where the sargassum weed drifts and the flying fishes soar like little silver birds.

There I encounter the charter fishermen in their able thirty-five-footers, with giant outriggers, with depth-finders, fathometers and ship-to-shore telephones. I know what they are telling their tourist fishermen in the cockpit: that I don't belong out there, I am a damned fool to be messing around in the Stream in a cockle-shell, that I will be caught in a blow some time and never get back—but I couldn't care less. As they are contemptuous of me, so I am contemptuous of them. The tourists who have paid $100 for a day's fishing have bought the skills and equipment of others. They will doubtless catch fish, but not the way I will, because I am my own man, running my own boat, beating down and landing my own fish. I feel smug and superior.

A reel screams and I grab the outfit, which is baited with a strip of mackerel belly. Nudging the outboard handle with my waist, I start the boat in a circle and fight down a shimmering blue-green bonito of about ten pounds. Just as I am reaching for the gaff, a triangular fin comes slicing in and I catch a glimpse of the body of a large shark as it comes charging in to gulp down the fish.

I hope that I will reel in just the bonito's head, but the shark is solidly hooked, and just for the hell of it I decide to fight him down. I "rev up" the outboard, clutch the rod with my knees and one hand, and off we go in a half-hour chase that ends in a stand-off, with the shark holding its ground about forty feet off the boat.

I shut off the engine and drift, the better to take a look at this sea tiger I have beaten down, taking out my knife to cut the line. It is a lemon shark of about 500 pounds, and as I eye it the shark is coldly eyeing me in circles that take it around and around the boat.

Sharks attract sharks and soon there are four or five joined in the circle and along with them the "friends of the sharks," a school of cobia or ling running 10 to 15 pounds each. There is a symbiosis between the cobia and the shark. Although the cobia will "take up" and swim along with manta rays and loggerheads, its strange friendship with the shark is dominant.

I dearly love cobia, fried in crisp fingers, so I stick the shark outfit under my right shoulder, pick up a medium-sized casting outfit already armed with a spoon, flick it out and catch three. The last one is too big to rassle aboard by the leader, so I grab a gaff, relax my shoulder and elbow clamp on the shark outfit, and the shark lunges, taking off with a heavy duty trolling outfit.

The "free roaming" frontier of the sea is rewarding. Next day at the newspaper office, when my associates ask me "Did you catch anything?" I say: "Learned a new way to catch cobia."

23

The Cleaning Station Is a Beginning of Sea Civilization

Immersed in the clear sea, a man is close to elemental beginnings. He moves with the surges that have pulsed against the land since life began.

The reef is a barrier against the surges, but a feeble one. It is built-in defiance of the sea by one of the myriad forms of life that came out of it.

There are reefs of many kinds in the tropics of the world, some made by coral polyps and some by the incalculable casting aside of the shells of mollusks and the skeletons of sea plumes. Most reefs are the bones of the countless generations of their builders, but not this one.

Our reef that stretches from Seminole Shores down to what is known as The Hole off Hobe Sound is built by worms, one grain of sand at a time. Billions upon billions of tiny red marine worms—the current wave of myriad generations—are building the live reef, with its

hummocks, mounds, grottoes and its plateaus.

In some places the reef is a few feet across and in others it is several hundred yards; it stretches from the shoreline for eight miles to the southward, where it is more than half a mile off land. Considering the size of the creatures that built it, our worm reef is a colossal work, dwarfing the Great Wall of China or the cities of men.

I floated in a grotto of the reef on a low tide at sundown. The newspaper, the town, the people and the world of men were far away. The sea came breaking in a few yards off upon the wall that the worms had built and the surges moved me in the pool with a delightful weightlessness.

The creatures of the pool hid at my coming, but they got used to me. The blennies and the wrasses were the first to come out from the rocks and give me the once-over. I hung suspended like a resting fish and the blennies became pugnacious, puffing out their gills and darting forward. "War or peace?" they seemed to ask.

A colorful Beau Gregorie flashed out to chase a blennie and cut back into its hiding place. Then out came a pair of brilliant sapphire-blue neon gobies like flecks of blue fire. And I saw a slender stick-candy-striped claw waving at me from a recess. Then I knew just where I was.

The grotto was a cleaning station, a place of truce in the vast reef. The little neon gobies and the candy-striped banded shrimp had mistaken me for a customer needing a cleaning job.

On the flood tide, when the swells would come in deep over the reef, there would be parrot fish, margates and groupers coming to call. They would lie suspended in the pool, head up, tail down, drifting at ease while the cleaning squad performed its job of removing parasites from gills and mouths and scales.

In the sea the swift and the merciless are forever pursuing something smaller. But in this grotto of the great wall that the worms have built, a grain of sand at a time, there is a peace of convenience. Here the fierce moray eel will come out of its hole, open its mouth and the little blue neon gobie will go fearlessly inside, plucking a tidbit from under a tongue. He serves.

The delectable red-banded shrimp—and I'm sure he must be delicious, because all shrimp are—will explore the gills and mouth of a grouper and instead of becoming a meal, will be paid off by being furnished with a meal for his labors. He works—for pay.

The cleaning station is an example of enlightened self-interest. The predators are willing to declare a truce if the little creatures serve them. The gobies and the red-banded shrimp and the wrasses are not "just good to eat"; but they are "good" in a higher category so well understood by men. They are useful.

The red-banded shrimp waved his claw, still offering to come out and assist me, and I said: "No thanks, buddy, but I sure appreciate the offer. It is noble of you."

The feigned altruism of my little friends palled. There is something hollow about people or creatures who are always offering to do something for others. I notice that they didn't venture near one corner of the pool where there was a pile of cracked crab shells in front of a dark hole.

Good! My confidence in the sea was restored. Shortly, when the sun went down, the octopus would leave his lair and lash out at all that cooperative bunch. He would make them run and hide and to hell with their simpering offers of help. " 'Service above Self,' my eye!" is his view. "The old ways are best."

And perhaps they are. The cleaning station has the glimmers of the beginning of a civilization, which could become so complicated that the simple sea should be saved the trouble. It is so much easier if things are just good to eat.

24

The Slow Manatee in Our Fast Times

The manatee or sea cow, placid, inoffensive, resembling a small walrus without tusks, still survives in Florida but its herds are vastly reduced and its chances made slim—unintentionally, of course—by the express cruiser and high speed outboard.

A computer analyzing the projected paths of manatees and their descendants and the coming courses of the thousands of fast pleasure craft of Florida's inland waters would find future collision points until it finally ran out of manatees.

Our spacious bays, their bottoms covered with manatee grass, were favored feeding grounds for the huge vegetarians up and down the St. Lucie. The bulls weigh several hundred pounds and an old cow can come close to a thousand. Manatee Pocket eastward of Port Salerno was named for the herds that used to graze there. Owen Murphy's Manatee Yacht Club Restaurant in that picturesque fishing town puts out attractive place mats with the sad figure of the oval tailed manatee on them, the closest that most visitors get to seeing one.

A herd going upstream in single file used to be a common sight in the lower bay down around Hell Gate. On such journeys, rolling to the top much like porpoises, they blow and dive. In proportion to its body, the manatee has a small head. A strung out herd of several on a cruise, glimpsed just at the instant when the leader has raised its head and the backs of the rest are arched above the surface, doubtless gave rise to the many reports of sighting "sea serpents over one hundred feet long."

The necessity to come up for air at regular intervals is the creature's undoing. Boats have been hitting manatees in Florida's bays ever since the days of sailboats and slow launches, but mostly all that resulted was bumps, alarmed boatmen and scared manatees.

When light rowboats and canoes were used more frequently than now, the manatee often got its revenge. There is tremendous power in that big, broad paddle of a tail. I have rowed over a manatee in the shallows and had it knock the rowboat a couple of feet in air with the force of a small marine mine exploding. Charles and Helen Schilling of Jensen Beach were thrown into the water and a flailing manatee tail broke the ribs of their canoe when they passed over one.

In what some of us still fondly call "the old days," the manatee was harpooned in the river for food by the pioneer settlers. They claimed that various parts of it, cut into roasts, chops and steaks, had the flavor of beef, veal, pork and lamb. Old ones tasted like manatee. After wise laws were passed to protect the creature, a hidden exploitation went on for many years by die-hard descendants of the old families who refused to give up roast of manatee. The docile creatures would be hemmed in by the giant black seines in the St. Lucie's bays. Most of the time—especially in daylight—the seiners would push down the corklines and ease the manatees over to freedom. They are pathetically non-resistant when trapped in a net and I have watched a netter put thumb and finger in a big manatee's nostrils and lead it gently over the corkline.

But often in the night the temptation would be too great. The manatee would be pole-axed, towed to a secret place upriver and butchered. I know of two or three of those ancient manatee butchering grounds up hidden mangrove creeks on the North Fork where, if you look closely, you can still find the curved ribs of sea cows slaughtered long ago. The ribs are "solid ivory" and make excellent knife handles.

The manatee has limpid brown eyes and an almost human face. When it sticks its head above water and sighs, taking in air, one realizes what founded the myth of the mermaids. The females give birth to their young in the far upper rivers, holding them close with their flippers and suckling them on two breasts.

With the disappearance of the manatee grass over much of their habitat, the manatees took to dining on shoreline growth and the water hyacinths that plague Florida's fresh and upper brackish reaches. Hearing that the dugong, a species of manatee, was being used successfully to cut down on water growth in the canals of Indonesia, Central and Southern Florida Flood Control District tried to put them to work in its canal system.

Hyacinths and other water weeds are constantly choking the canals and it is tremendously expensive to remove them by chemical or mechanical means. The transported manatees, placed in interior canals, went to work with a will in the first stages of the experiment, munching hyacinths like crazy—and everybody was happy.

However, they could stand pure fresh water just so long. Some clock within the manatees' bodies signaled that it was time to go to sea again. They were blocked by dams when they attempted passage downstream and succumbed to a cold winter in the chilled canal waters.

If computers could talk they might say: "Enjoy yourselves, manatees, while you may."

25

The Virtues of Rising Early in Our Hectic Days

The beauty of the morning is one of the most rewarding things about South Florida's late spring and early summer. It starts getting light these days around 5:15 with the "false dawn" and from then until around 7:30 the new day arrives.

I like to time myself so that I start my engine and feel my way down Manatee Pocket in time to meet the sunrise at St. Lucie Inlet. With a green flood tide rushing in and a majestic stage setting of pink tinted clouds to the east, pierced by shafts of light, one has the feeling of setting out on a great adventure.

Before the sun has had time to warm the land, the air is usually still and cool; you can be fairly sure that there will not be any dangerous winds before 8:30 at least—and if there is such a chance, black squall clouds will give you ample warning.

On some summer mornings the sea is exceptionally

clear. The whole St. Lucie reef, to the north and to the south, is a vast aquarium in which drift exotic angelfish, triggerfish, giant rays, groupers and sharks. A drama of life and death unfolds before you as you cruise: mackerel and blues splashing at rain minnows, tiny balao getting up on their tails and skimming in advance of bonitos, the savage onslaught of a shark against an unsuspecting and unalert tarpon.

You are apt to see the majestic king mackerel hurl itself fifteen feet in air in a thirty-five foot arc while pursuing flying fish. There will be giant loggerheads lolling on the surface, waiting for the full moon to spawn upon the beaches. I am told by one of our veteran commercial fishermen that there is one reef over which you can drift and count the cannon row on row of a long-foundered man of war. I do not know where it is nor do I care to know, because it seems to me that such history is better locked under the sea than brought out, daubed with aluminum paint and placed in a park or a museum.

One of the great sights of the morning is the seabirds winging out to get their breakfasts. All veteran fishermen watch the birds and where the gulls go, there go they.

Also, almost unconsciously, all ocean fishermen watch each other. Has a boat off toward the horizon stopped? That means it has tied into a fish. Watch it a while longer; does it start up and stop again? That means it is most apt to be in a school of big kings. Your veteran sea fisherman can catch the glint of a boated mackerel five miles away and when he sees it repeated three or four times, he heads that way.

The first two hours after dawn are usually the most active in the day; porpoises roll and feed, in fact everything is after breakfast—and, in warmer months, you can pack a lot of action in the three hours between 5:30 and 8:30, be back at the dock by 9 with a fine catch.

Early morning is equally fascinating and productive on our fresh waters. You'll see sandhill cranes strolling, without their usual fear, cottontail rabbits by the side of the sand trails, grey and fox squirrels, and the fresh water fish, like their salty cousins, want breakfast too.

There are rare exceptions, when "the moon is wrong," as the Crackers say, when there is no sign of activity at dawn. The birds aren't feeding and the fish aren't biting. When you hit those periods, you might as well go home. Nothing on earth that I know of will make a fish bite during those "super-dead" periods. I have actually grabbed a leopard frog and thrown it out into a clear lake where I could see half a dozen bass lolling on such a day and they paid no more attention to it than if it had been a stick or a leaf.

The more people we get and the more boat traffic which develops as a consequence, the smarter it is to get out there real early.

St. Lucie Canal is a case in point. From dawn to 8 a.m. when the St. Lucie Lock opens, there is comparatively little boat traffic and you can get in a couple of hours of pleasant and productive casting.

After the parade of speedboats, express cruisers, shrimpers and tugboats starts passing through, wakes come crashing in against the banks, the water becomes roiled and discolored, and your fishing is through until evening.

I like my mornings quiet and peaceful, as they used to be. The only way I know to get them is to get up early before this pandemonium that we call civilization arrives in the outdoors.

One morning recently I learned the hard way what happens if you don't. I was fishing the Indian River shortly before noon, when about twenty racing speedboats zoomed by, one after another, two airplanes buzzed me, and it seemed to me that there was not one second in an hour that I could not hear the high pitched whine of outboards racing madly, while my boat rocked and tossed from their wakes. That, for me, is not fun; from now on I'm an early bird.

26

The Fisherman Is a Happy Man in Early Morning

The fisherman loves to row out in the stillness of the mists of the morning when the lake is like polished black glass.

He rows slowly and silently in the hush of the birth of the day, feathering the oars with a twist of his wrists. It is marvelous that the boat moves, even when he rests the oars in the air—and he thinks of the victory so long ago when men found that they could move over water on a floating log. Fun then began.

Two Florida mallards, with five bits of fluffy yellow down behind them, move as effortlessly as he does up the lake shore and the drake swings protectively to the rear. There were a dozen ducklings to start with, the fisherman thinks—seeing in his mind a snake stealing an egg or two, a snapping turtle taking its toll, a black bass having a duckling for breakfast.

The family of ducks disappears, melting into sedge as

149

the red ball of the sun pushes over the mists of the flatwoods. "I came from there," thinks the fisherman. "How ridiculous and mysterious and miraculous that everything on this earth was torn from that star. Say, that looks good," he says to himself.

What looks good and what looks bad to a fisherman would not be understood by other men. His perceptions are deep. He thinks like a fish. He views the lilypads, the sedge, the coves, the points of land, the snags, the little recesses, and he thinks: "If I were a fish, I would be right there."

He looks in past the lilypads to a little lane on the surface through them that leads to a sort of hidey-hole against a deep cutbank—and that is the sort of a place where he would be lurking if he were a fish. He would be ready to snap up a grasshopper that fell from the willows, a hapless frog or a careless shiner. Suddenly he knows that there is a fish there and a good one, just because he knows it. That is the way fishermen are.

"I will have a hard time getting him out of there," he tells himself. "He will tie me up in the lilypad stems, but nothing ventured, nothing gained." He is an optimist and daring pessimist combined.

The fisherman is an artist. All his life he has developed his skills. He may not be the best, but he is one of the best, and that is a satisfaction. Last night he greased his line and put a touch of graphite on it so that it would slide slickly through the guides. He opened the bend of the hooks on his flies so that they would work just a trifle better than the manufacturer made them and he honed the points of the hooks until they were like needles. Perfection is a matter of trifles and the fisherman is a perfectionist.

He false-casts with the fast action fly rod over his shoulder—again and a littler higher—and then he places the bass bug with its twitching rubber band legs exactly where he wants it, way back in the hidey-hole, two inches from the bank. He lets it lie still. Then he twitches the fly line, bringing the bug forward six inches and letting it rest again. "Hit it! Hit it! Hit it!" thinks the fisherman, as if by sheer mind-power he could conjure the fish he has imagined is there into striking the deceptive artificial bug.

No dice. Maybe it is too early for grasshoppers to fall into the water, thinks the fisherman. He snips off the bass bug and ties on a split tailed streamer. The lure is a thing of feathers and it does not look like a frog until the fisherman drops it back into the hidey-hole and gives it a twitch. Then its split white hackle opens and closes like a pair of tiny frog legs. The fisherman watches it, opening and closing a couple of inches under the water. It blacks out and he strikes.

The black bass charges out through the little lane in the lilypads. It is going to be a good morning, thinks the fisherman, desperately pulling in slack, grabbing an oar with one hand and giving it a pull, switching the rod and giving a heave to the other oar. It is good luck that the bass is heading for open water and he must head for open water, too. "Give me room," prays the fisherman, "lots of room to play him. He is a big one."

The big bass—and he is a beauty—comes to the top, half out, and shakes his open mouth and rattles his gills. He is too big to jump all the way out, like smaller bass. "Oh, what a bass!" thinks the fisherman, his heart beating fast. A redwinged blackbird bursts into liquid song over the bulrushes. Three sandhill cranes fly over the lake shattering the stillness with their rattling cacophony.

The fisherman does not hear the one or see the others. He is a happy man and it is a beautiful morning.

27

My Little Boat Named Lulu Has Really Lived

My boat Lulu has really lived. She is a trim little gal, eight feet from bow to stern with a three and a half foot beam. Sharp bowed and square sterned, she has numbers of holes drilled along her gunwales, the better for lines to be tied to saw grass or bonnets—and for stringers to hang from.

Despite her more than 40 years, Lulu is sound as the day she was made. She is bone-dry, light and able, and responds to the oars like a duck swimming to feed.

And it is beyond any sensible calculation how many black bass have been caught from Lulu.

Ernie Ricou ordered the little pond boat made—by eye and without plans—by a master seine boat builder at Jensen around 1925 for just one purpose, catching big black bass in the Savannas and Henderson Pond.

Ernie used a battery of long cane poles armed with stout lines, big corks and strong hooks baited with live

bluegills when he fished from Lulu. He used only big live baits for the biggest of bass. Black bass fishing was sort of a "sailor-rowing-in-the park" holiday for him because Ernie ran one of the biggest fish houses on the Indian River in Jensen.

It was not unusual for the Ricou fish house to ice down and ship 20,000 to 30,000 pounds of mullet, sea trout, pompano and bottomfish in a day, scooped up by giant nets from the salty Indian River. But, in the midst of all those fish, Ernie dreamed of getting away to bass fish from Lulu on the lilypad speckled fresh waters of the Savannas.

And did he catch bass! Ernie landed literally hundreds of eight to fourteen pound largemouths from Lulu in the years that he owned her. In a weak moment, he sold her to my father, Harry Lyons, and Dad carved his initials in her stern.

My father was one of the redoubtable pond fishermen of this part of Florida. Fresh water fishing was his life and, even in his old age, he managed to get Lulu transported to the Savannas, Mile Lake and dozens of nameless little ponds where the big bass lurked. Dad was a past master of all the arts, skills and trickeries by which bass are lured by men and he used them all from Lulu, adding his numbers to the legions that had been caught by Ernie.

But one day Lulu disappeared, stolen from a bayhead where she had been hidden. A couple of years went by before I got a hint that it just might be that a certain alligator hunter, spotlighting 'gators at night, was using a boat I might be interested in. I don't say it was Lulu, nor just how I stole Lulu back, but the boat I got back was remarkably like Lulu.

My son, growing up, took quite a fancy to Lulu. Whoever had taken the boat "into custody" had carved out Dad's initials from the stern. Bill· put his on the bow, where they are today, "W. L." He used her on Mile Lake, up Bessey Creek, to reach hidden, secret waters, and even occasionally upon the wide St. Lucie, although I worried when he did.

Lulu was a temptation to the young. One day two boys untied her from the bank and made off upriver. One fell overboard and drowned just north of the Stuart Bridge. That was sad. I have always felt badly about it. They would have been more than welcome to have had the pleasure of paddling Lulu in the shallows—but, in their innocence, they did not know the dangers in wide waters. From then on, I kept her in the backyard.

In his later years, Ernie Ricou asked if he could buy Lulu back. "No," I said, "but I'll lend her to you for as long as you want to use her." He enjoyed the little boat again until he was no longer able to fish.

I thought of all the pleasure Lulu had given a succession of fishermen the other day when I spent the weekend camping with Harry Dyer, Jim Pomeroy, Mike Littman and Guy Boyd at their hidey-hole in the deep piney woods. I took the little boat along in the back of the station wagon.

Their camp is near a beautiful blue eyed pond where I fished all day from Lulu. I watched flocks of swallows dipping, flights of egrets, a fish hawk wheeling and sandhill cranes flying over whooping it up. Enjoyed myself real good. Caught fish, too.

Judge Dyer is a superb camp cook and he turned out heaping portions of bream and bass that night, dipped in corn meal and fried to a golden brown, with hot grits and butter on the side.

I dropped off to sweet dreams early. Harry told the others next morning that he had heard me muttering, "You're a sweet old girl, Lulu," when he passed my cot just before daybreak to start breakfast.

It couldn't be. No fisherman in his right mind could fall in love with a boat.

28

Being Useless Has Advantages for a Mudfish

Being useless has its advantages. Last Saturday afternoon I went "back-country fishing" on a canal that borders Allapattah Road, in the western part of the county. "How did you do?" asked a friend. "Didn't catch anything. Scored a blank," I replied.

That was both true and untrue. I did not catch anything useful or esteemed. After an hour of fruitless casting, I did get a tremendous strike from a very large fish. I was deeply disappointed when it lunged to the surface, threw its body half out of water and I saw that it was a mudfish or grinnel.

It was a very big mudfish, close to twelve pounds, and it fought like a tiger. My red dog Pudge came running down to the canal edge to see its master conquer another of the lesser creatures. My wife, who had been reading a newspaper in our car parked nearby, took time out to remark: "You've really got a big one, haven't you?" "Yep," I replied, playing the fish with only one hope—that I could save the plug.

No fisherman plays a black bass with the hope that he can save the plug. He would gladly give a hundred plugs to hang on to a twelve pound bass. Even if he lost it, he would tell again and again how the noble fish came to the surface and tried to shake the lure.

Black bass are good. They are honorable, esteemed, and even useful. You can win fishing contests with them. You can brag about them. You can eat even the biggest, baked with bacon strips and tomato sauce to disguise the bassy taste. Anglers have been known to pay taxidermists outrageous fees to mount twelve pound black bass to gather dust on the living room wall until the day when their wives give them to the trash men. Black bass are very good.

But mudfish are "No-goodniks." They are the Al Capones of the fresh water fishing world. I do not know what mudfish do in their spare time, but I suspect that they carry crooked dice and burn their draft cards.

My mudfish was a dirty fighter. He bored into tree stumps, piles of brush and floating hyacinths. Once he threw his body all the way out on the opposite bank. If he had been a black bass, I would have lost him right then.

He was both useless and unlosable. When I finally had him at my feet, pulled all the way out on the bank, I carefully cut my plug from his lips, picked him up and threw him 15 feet out into the canal.

My dog looked at me in amazement. My wife called

from the car: "Did you lose that big fish?" "Yep," I said. "He broke my line."

The white lie that the mudfish had broken my line was intended to cover up the fact that my encounter had been with so ignoble a foe.

I did not catch anything else, but the more I think about that useless mudfish the more I realize that he has it made.

Nobody wants to catch him, nobody desires to brag about his fighting abilities. No one will ever tote him to a taxidermist and order him mounted. He has probably been thrown back dozens of times by anglers who did not care to mention it and he can look forward to more of the same.

Being utterly useless, no good for anything, scorned by the fishing fraternity, all add up to immunity and longevity for the mudfish. From his viewpoint, uselessness must be the best thing in this world.

29

Lazy Minutes in a Garden, Just Wasting Time

Sitting still, being quiet, just watching is an art. Try sitting in a garden, indulging in the most absolute laziness, observing and speculating without purpose or plan.

To heck with cleaning the yard, oiling my fishing tackle, painting the boat, clearing out the garage or any of those nuisance jobs that use spare time constructively. I indulge in the greatest of all luxuries: deliberately wasting precious time.

I sit under our spreading old Mulgoba mango tree whose forefathers came from India, enjoying its dappled shade—and, in my mind's eye I see monkeys in its branches and holy men pausing to rest in the comfort of its shadows.

There is movement in the branches—not a monkey but a saucy grey squirrel, tail flicking, coming down the bole to pilfer a jawful of the fluffy sphagnum moss I have packed around the roots of a giant staghorn fern whose forefathers came from New Guinea. The squirrel and its mate are building a nest high in the tree. Coming is another generation of squirrels to be born naked and helpless in a cozy home, soft and dry, protected by love.

We human beings talk of love as if we had a monopoly on it, but the cow loves her calf, the cat her kittens, the gorilla her child. There are many Madonnas enclosed in the strange shapes of prisons of flesh, but we are too stingy to admit it. Love is not ours alone; it is universal among the warm blooded.

The staghorn fern came to Florida from the rain forests of tropical lands—and I have species from Java, Ethiopia, Australia, South Africa and the Amazon. Don't ask me why. Some people collect playing cards. I collect Platyceriums, just because I like them. Like the lady who started collecting pancakes and wound up with a whole trunk full, I have a dozen species all busily having "puppies" around the shields of their spreading fronds. They throw forward the torch of the future of their kind. Is there love in them, too?

Sitting in my garden, observing my collection of exotic ferns, there comes to my mind a vision of something I have always wanted, never been able to get. I want a fish that is 50,000,000 years old, its skeleton delicately impressed upon a piece of slate. The natural history museums have thousands of them. Why can't I have one?

How could I possibly secure a fossilized fish?—but the thought is interrupted by a movement of green on one of the pendant staghorn fronds. It is a little green chameleon, hunting insect prey. He hops to the bark of the tree and turns brown. So there aren't any miracles any more? You try doing it.

The chameleon reminds me of Tyrannosaurus Rex, the most terrible of dinosaurs, the flesh eater who used to pounce on the huge, slow, vegetation eating dinosaurs of his time. A blue jay spots me and starts cussing me out. "You, too," I think, "came up from the line of the flying lizards, are a cousin of the chameleon."

A beautiful yellow and black swallowtail butterfly flits through the garden, a creature that flaps and falls and rises—it never really learned to fly like the houseflies and the bees that defy all aeronautical rules. And there's a black and yellow carpenter bee, which isn't a bee at all but a fly that imitates the bumble bee. Why yellow and black? I don't know, except that those colors in combination are avoided by all insect eating birds. Those are the colors of greatest safety in the airy world of eat or be eaten.

A movement on the ground attracts my eye. A wasp is doggedly dragging a caterpillar many times its weight toward a little hole in the soil. It has stung and paralyzed the caterpillar, tugs it down into the hole, will lay on its back an egg that will turn into a grub that will eat the host alive—and become a wasp to do it all over again. The wasp contrives to feed its young. Is that an act of love?

There are worm casts on top of the ground and I think of the thousands upon thousands of worms—such fine fish bait—that are devouring the fallen leaves of the mango tree and turning them into richer soil.

How many living creatures are there in my garden,

where I sit "alone" observing? Not counting the catbirds that scratch covertly in fallen leaves, not counting the flashing little hummingbirds that take nectar from the red flowers of the firecracker plants, not counting the worms or the grubs of beetles hibernating just underground, there are billions and quadrillions.

There are spores of moulds and mushrooms filling the air, all eagerly seeking a favored spot to recreate their kind. Every cubic foot of the topsoil has countless billions of bacteria eating away at organic material, dividing and recreating themselves. There are more living creatures in my garden than there are human beings on the planet and each is important to itself.

"Oh there you are," my wife calls from the back porch. "What are you doing?"

"Just sitting," I reply. "Doing nothing." But to myself I add "and having a wonderful time."

30

South Florida's Seasons Change as Everywhere

The seasons do change in South Florida—but you have to live here quite a while to recognize just how.

Even without a touch of frost, the swamp maples put on a grand display of red and yellow painted leaves with the coming of winter and the leaves of our native dwarf hickories turn brown and fall.

The moss hung cypress trees in our swamps drop all their leaves and we know it's spring when their first greenery reappears.

Winter is signalled by the coming, not the going, of vast flocks of robins which feast on the red berries of the pepper trees and practically denude the cabbage palms of their black berries. Don't worry about the future of pepper and palm trees; the robins plant them by the millions all over the land.

We know it's winter, too, when the vast flocks of bluebill ducks form rafts in the broad bays of the St.

Lucie. Migrating fish signal the change of the seasons, blues, mackerel and kings in winter, and tarpon and snook in summer.

If someone tells you that vast schools of mullet are coming down St. Lucie Canal from Lake Okeechobee headed for the sea you don't have to look at your calendar to know that it is in the second week of December. A wonderful clock inside the mullet signals every year that it is time to rush to the sea and spawn.

Should you read in *The News* that "jumbo snook are feeding on huge schools of dog faced eels in the North Fork Bay," don't bother to check the date of the paper. It will be in the last week of June, whether the year is 1968 or 1970.

In early winter hosts of migratory songbirds take advantage of the feeders in our yards and we get them again on their way back north. You'll know it's late spring when, all of a sudden, the shrubs in your garden are full of tiny, twittering birds, the last contingent of the northbound flights. Along about then the hummingbirds appear, bound northward from South America.

The long time Floridian is more conscious of the change of the seasons simply because he knows the country better. He watches the sandhill cranes do their stately courtship dance, observes the grey squirrels building their new nests in the Florida spruce—those trees on the sand ridges that always lean the way of the wind—and knows that the universal time of raising new families is under way.

The spring flowers of Florida are unobtrusive. They don't smack you in the eye. But, if you will look, they are there—the flower stalks of the palms, the colorful tiger lily, the delicate little ground orchids and their arboreal kin. That flash of red high in the water oak is the spike of a crimson flowered air plant.

Our wild grapes ripen earlier than they do in the north. If you know where they are, you can gather buckets of delicious wild grapes in the old pineapple fields during July and early August. Fox grapes, too, are abundant in that season along the upper rivers.

Right now mid-winter is the time chosen by the beautiful African tulip trees to bloom. In February and March the lavender flowered jacarandas will put on their annual display. And the most flamboyant of them all, the Royal Poinciana, naked all winter, becomes umbrella-shaped masses of red and orange orchid-like blossoms in June.

Our seasons are pretty reliable. You can depend on June being the best month of the year, although a little warm. From July through October, there just might be a hurricane, a hazard shared from Texas to New England.

Right now in January is the most undependable season of all. Remembering the freeze of 1964, most Floridians have stocked up on firewood, fuel oil and liquid gas. They do this despite the fact that the tourists are walking around in play suits and Bermuda shorts displaying sunburned knees and noses.

Should a blue norther come romping down, with icicles on the shrubbery in Stuart's parks and tourists wearing overcoats, even a Floridian will know that winter has arrived. We've been spared that sort of winter so far this year. Just so you'll recognize it, here's what one is like: It warms up, it rains, it turns bitter cold, it warms up, it rains, it turns cold again. Remember?

31

A Florida Garden Offers Retirees a Bonus of Fun

Working with the land is the most rewarding of all hobbies.

While I have no quarrel with it, I'm frankly puzzled by the apartment sales pitch that: "You'll have no more yard problems."

Problems? They must mean fun. There are no problems connected with a yard or even a few acres of living space around a home unless you make them yourself by putting in too much lawn.

Admittedly, it can be a chore if you want your yard to resemble the sweeping green of a fancy golf course. But why do that? There is plenty of low growing ground cover adaptable to South Florida which requires no mowing at all. Some even have a profusion of flowers to delight the eye.

My advice to retirees coming to this part of South Florida is to buy fun space for those leisure years. You

173

don't have to settle for little cookie cutter houses on narrow lots jammed shoulder to shoulder with one continuous lawn.

If you do a little careful looking around, you can buy an acre or two or several contiguous lots and have room for your own orange, tangerine and grapefruit trees. All they require is a couple of applications of fertilizer each year, a spraying or two—and there's real satisfaction in going out and picking your own grapefruit for breakfast.

One of the fastest growing of Florida backyard fruits is the papaya, called "paw-paw" by the old-timers. You can have bearing papaya trees in a year to 14 months after planting and some of the varieties are simply delicious.

There are species of peaches acclimated to the sub-tropics which grow well in South Florida, but much more satisfactory are the superior varieties of mango, such as the Haden or Mulgoba. These have a peach-like flavor and are wonderful with sugar and cream.

Do you miss the raspberries of Wisconsin? A hedge of tropical black raspberries is the Florida substitute. Yes, you can have a strawberry patch here and, if you go in for serious vegetable gardening, you can grow snap beans in six weeks, tomatoes, mustard greens and other fine table fare during the cooler months, if you have room.

One year I got the yen to grow Kentucky Wonder pole beans, went out on the bank of St. Lucie Canal and cut a couple of hundred maiden-cane poles. I crossed these poles and tied their tops together tepee-style in four twenty-foot rows, planted the beans and watched them climb, flower and produce more than we could eat.

Both my wife and I love to garden in our spare time, and we are busy people. Her hobby is orchids, which take only an occasional spraying and repotting under shade in a slat-house. They grow on you. You get the "orchid bug." Hardly a week goes by now all year around without the little orchid house producing a spray of flamboyant beauty to be enjoyed on our porch. My chief garden hobby is more selective, being centered on Platyceriums or staghorn ferns from the tropics of the world. I get a big bang out of growing under the old mango tree these exotic ferns from Java, Australia and the South American jungles.

And what do you think I found under the Christmas tree? It was a great big book called *Exotica*, listing and illustrating just about every exotic plant in the world! A book like that makes you wish you had more land to try to see if more and more of these species will grow in South Florida.

I can easily understand how Ed Menninger got hooked on his flowering tree hobby until he had imported the seeds of more than 3,000 species and acclimated a couple of hundred of them to South Florida. What a gift of beauty he has made to Stuart, Ft. Myers and scores of other communities where these bouquets of the giants now landscape roadways and beautify private yards.

When you settle in South Florida, try to acquire enough open space so you can have the added pleasure of gardening. Old fashioned tea roses grow and bloom here prolifically all year around. There are things to learn—the sandy soil needs mulching and watering and our ornamental shrubs do best planted close together for company—but there's fun in learning, too.

What I'm taking so long trying to say is really simple. You don't have to shut yourself up in a tight little air conditioned cubicle with a shirt tail patch of Bermuda grass around it just because some developers think that's the Florida way of life.

You can throw open the doors and windows to the breeze and get outside and enjoy the sun, the clean air, the birds and the garden. Believe me, it's no "problem," just a bonus of fun.

32

Having Fun Is an Important Part of Living Here

This is still one of the few places in the U.S.A. where a fellow can make a living—and take a $500 vacation each weekend for a few bucks.

There comes to mind a printer on *The Stuart News*, Dalton Anderson, a family man with multifold responsibilities, who makes up ads, sets heads and is generally well occupied throughout the week.

In this respect, Mr. Anderson is not much different from thousands of printers in hundreds of newspaper composing rooms throughout the nation. He works, but after work, on his day off, Mr. Anderson has the edge on the working population less fortunately situated.

Before dawn, he hitches the family chariot to a seaworthy, twin-outboard trailer boat in the carporte of his home and in half an hour, as the sun comes up over the Gulf Stream, he is out on the blue water, apt as not to be battling a sailfish, a king mackerel, or loading the

177

boat with bluefish.

The fish he catches probably do not cost him more per pound than prime sirloin steak. If you caught them as a tourist, flying down and hiring a charter craft, the cost would be by the carat.

On those mornings, he is the captain of his ship, often host to visiting fishing writers, his own youngsters, friends and kinfolk from abroad. We can not help but compare him to a printer in Chicago, New York or some other unblessed urban sprawl.

He is only one of the many here who take full advantage of the fact that South Florida is a place to have fun—without waiting for that annual two week vacation, without having to spend two days on the road, without having to buy plane tickets or make reservations at a resort.

Having fun is the most important part of living here. If you aren't having your share, you are cheating yourself. The happiest people we know make a point of enjoying themselves in their spare time in ways too many to list here.

Having fun may mean joining the Audubon Society and widening your horizons on Florida birdlife or joining Stuart Garden Club and the Men's Garden Club of Martin County and meeting kindred spirits in the field of gardening.

There's no telling where fun hobbies can lead you in Martin County. Take Edwin A. Menninger as a shining example. Ed became interested in flowering trees, started introducing them to Florida from tropical lands around the world, began writing and publishing books about them—and now he is an eminent world authority on tropical flowering trees.

The Francis Pelosis, a husband and wife team at Jensen Beach, became interested in shell collecting and the making of shell jewelry as a fun pursuit. Their hobby grew into a business and into the publication of a book which ranks them with top Florida authorities.

Elmer De Witt, a plumber, became interested in growing tropical orchids, and now he's building a thriving commercial orchid business. Paul Mahan, retired postmaster at Hobe Sound, turned to the hobby of growing tropical fruits in an organic garden and succeeded so well that he was featured recently in a national gardening magazine.

Kenneth Wright, who used to run a small shop in Stuart, got fun out of an aquarium which he stocked with tropical fish, began raising them in pools at his home, bought acreage out in the country and went into it on a big scale. His fun hobby has grown until he is now one of Florida's largest wholesale suppliers of tropical fish.

Pat Sullivan was a radio and TV personality in the mad whirl of the Miami—Fort Lauderdale complex until he moved to Stuart where, for fun, he expanded his "rockhound" hobby. He and his wife have developed a jewelry business on their own, making practically everything they sell—turning fun into a business that lets them take long summer jaunts "rockhounding."

Those are only a few instances in which having fun hit the jackpot. They're mentioned because fun seekers and hobbyists should be forewarned to limit their enthusiasms.

We know one fellow who is pretty much soured off

at "fun in the sun." He was a busy Middle West executive who never had time or space to indulge in his hobby of growing roses. He bought a few acres in Martin County, started setting out rose plants, began shipping roses North "and now I don't have time for anything but these dratted roses," he complains.

So have fun. But use moderation. There's no sense in becoming a business success and then letting a little innocent fun turn you into another business success all over again.

You might try clam squirt watching. This involves sitting on the beach at low tide and seeing which clam can spit the farthest. You can take a stop-watch and determine the exact ratio of variance in the intervals between clam squirts. It's quiet, restful fun and we haven't heard yet of anyone getting rich at it.

33

The Florida Dream Compared to the Florida Reality

In the minds of millions Florida has become a dream land to which they will retire some day, solving all problems and living happily thereafter.

In candor, as a Florida country newspaperman, I feel impelled to say that this happy prospect is not always borne out by the facts. The Florida dream and Florida reality differ sharply.

Retirement to Florida sometimes produces a lemon instead of a juicy orange—and it is sad to see the old folks stuck with something bitter all the rest of their lives.

My sincere advice is that all prospective retirees go through a looking and waiting period before pulling up roots and transplanting themselves. Since the average retiree family, selling their home in some other state, has the finances for just one more move—that one move better be right.

The happiest retirees I know first put their toes in the water by vacationing around the state. They visited the East Coast and the West Coast, went up into the Panhandle and down into the Keys. They took their time, investigating the big cities, the planned communities and the small towns. They checked the long-term costs of various types of housing—cottages, homes, apartments, condominiums and mobile homes—and, most importantly, the sort of people they would be associated with and the community services which they would need for peace of mind and happiness.

Some of them settled here, some at Sarasota and Key West, in West Palm Beach or Miami but, without exception, those who feel they made a good move took their time. A number of them rented for a year before buying. They found out what groceries cost, clothing, fuel—and, most importantly, what to do with their spare time.

The unhappiest I know are some who dived abruptly into artificial situations. They bought in remote planned communities, where let's say a retired Army Colonel and his wife have as neighbors a retired Iowa farming couple. Even wearing sports shirts and slacks, never the twain shall really meet and understand each other. Both couples suffer the loneliness of having left their own sort of people.

While it is meant as an amusing crack, the saying, "Keep Florida green, bring money," should be beefed up to "bring enough money." Those who have retired on small pensions and Social Security often find that their income is not adequate to their needs. They have to skimp and save, look for outside jobs which are scarce and low-paid and they live in a constant fear of inflation and rising taxes. Sunshine and bathing beaches will not dispel the gloom of retiring to poverty. Be sure you are adequately financed.

And, unless you have a lot of money, forget about a home on the beach, riverfront or lakefront. If you can't afford a home in a deluxe subdivision where you now live, you won't be able to afford waterfront property in Florida. Many are able and they build beautiful places on the water with their own cruisers—but don't dream about it if you can't afford that type of living where you are now.

Retirees should be warned that just finding a home is only the first step. What are you going to do next? Look at each other all day? Just vegetating can result in one or both parties hitting the bottle, becoming morose old men or vitriolic old women. Are you going to go fishing all day while your wife sits home and watches TV? Brother, it won't work.

Again—back to that cream on top of the milk, the happy retirees—we suggest that finding an absorbing interest is primary. It may be a dedicated hobby like growing orchids, collecting sea shells, making driftwood furniture; or it may be an activity like helping out at the Chamber of Commerce, joining the Pink Ladies at the hospital, or volunteering to help at the public library. Mainly, it is doing something you want to do and like to do.

Some go to night classes, learn foreign languages they missed, or take real estate courses and become salesmen—sometimes mediocre, sometimes successful. Many become interested in art or color photography.

The artists show the best judgment in this connection because they retain more friends than those happy retirees who inflict two-hour slide shows on the unhappy neighbors.

Be extremely leery of investing in undeveloped Florida lots with the assurance that you are going to make money. Chances are that the developer has 100,000 more to sell before yours ever turn over again.

Yes, some retirees do come to Florida and make business successes, but far more lose their shirts, and it's tough to lose the nest egg when you can't lay any more. Family type motels are out. There's a huge mortality in small eating places. The gift shop deal has been overworked. Just because a car-wash is successful back home doesn't mean it will go over here.

Vacation in Florida, roam the state, rent a while and be just as cautious with your money here as you would be in Chicago. Our sharks are not all in the ocean. Don't overlook the hazards of Florida reality in making your Florida dream come true.

34
Happiness Is Teasing Bugs Out of Holes

There are many stages of happiness. Here is one of the first:

Happiness is teasing doodlebugs with a straw and jerking them out of their holes. My, aren't they surprised!

It is watching mullet jump just for the fun of it, enjoying life; and buzzards wheeling high without moving a wing, looking for death.

Happiness is a slice of crusty home made bread hot out of the oven, spread with butter and downed with a cold glass of milk.

Happiness is hot biscuits, country ham and red-eye gravy for breakfast.

It is bending down to drink from a cold mossy run on a hot day.

It is catching spotted leopard frogs with your bare hands and then letting them go.

Happiness is walking with your dog in the woods while he goes crazy pointing stink sparrows and box turtles and then flushes a real quail.

Happiness is your first cottontail to go in the pot.

It is running barefoot down a sand trail and jumping over bushes like a deer.

It is sitting still, looking at the moon and the stars and wondering.

Happiness is watching hunting hawks hovering, the soundless flight of an owl or the swift strike of a falcon.

It is learning by yourself that everything eats something a little smaller until the very biggest are eaten by the very smallest—which will get you some day, darn them!

Happiness is discovering that not everything the grown-ups say is true.

It is watching people when they don't know they are being watched.

It is catching your first fish and cooking it over your own coals and eating it with your fingers with a palmetto frond for a plate.

Happiness is realizing that you are you and there is nobody else in the wide creation exactly like you.

Happiness is when the stone bruises on your feet get replaced by callouses.

Happiness is coming home with a bucket of wild grapes for your mother to cook into jelly. It is killing your first rattlesnake after you darned near stepped on the bodacious varmint.

It is outwitting adult schemers by disappearing when they have something planned for you to do.

It is watching oysters spit and then outspitting them.

It is swinging out naked on a muscadine vine over the old swimming hole, grabbing your nose and letting go.

It is fights when you win them and those you lose are best forgotten.

It is a long, tall, cold ice cream soda sipped up a straw while your ankles are gripping the twisty wire legs of one of those old fashioned drugstore chairs.

At least, that's what happiness was. I'm mentioning it in case some of you old guys may have forgotten. A dime to a dollar, it's still there!

35

Take Time, Enjoy the Real Florida

Millions come to Florida—and never see it. They are like motorized pellets in a glamorized pinball machine, hitting the flashing lights of widely publicized artificial attractions before bouncing out of the state and back home.

Our beautiful natural springs, which might have been preserved as treasures of serenity, have been ballyhooed into carnivals with barkers in glass bottomed boats or exhibits of simpering underwater mermaids and performing seals.

Porpoise shows and reptile exhibits, alligator farms and deer parks, simulations of the African veldt with lions roaming at large, monkey and parrot jungles and water ski shows infest the state. A'building is Disney World, a vast complex in what till now was a pleasant wilderness of lakes and swamps, destined to put Disneyland to shame.

191

If that's your "thing," you can bounce from one to another on any of the main routes, visit all the commercial aquarium shows, see cobras milked and—if you have anything left—get milked yourself at a Miami Beach clip-joint.

But the Florida we love who have lived here most of our lives has no admission fee, except the desire to appreciate beauty, the awareness to see it and the time to enjoy it.

Our amazing shows are the wonders of ever changing clouds, low to the land, sometimes like placid white cattle grazing down a blue pasture, often in tumultuous thunderheads that boil in majesty or in threatening black line squalls. We love to watch them trailing skirts of rain across the saw grass swamps, cabbage palm hammocks and pine forests. If you came to Florida and didn't feel close to the clouds, you really didn't see Florida.

The real Florida is a land of beauty and serenity, a place to take time to enjoy dawns and sunsets beyond the river against silhouetted pines. It is a place to hear the wind in the needles of the pines and to remember the dancing wraiths of Spanish moss on live-oaks. Florida is for quiet contemplation on a sea beach, watching pelicans skimming the breakers in single file like long vanished pterodactyls.

Florida is for quiet fun, crabbing in the bays, catching shrimp from bridges and holding "shrimp boils" on the beach, catching whiting and yellow tail croaker in the surf and cooking them over a driftwood fire, going oystering and clamming. It is for walking and seeing and doing and having fun.

Florida is for amazement, wonder and delight, and refreshment of the soul. It may take a little more time to hunt out and enjoy the real Florida, but you will be well repaid.

Take time to feel the cathedral stillness of Corkscrew Swamp over near Immokalee, where centuries old cypresses will speak if you can hear. Take time to go deep into a South Florida hammock and see fragile wild orchids. Visit Everglades National Park and marvel at the vast rookeries in the brooding mangrove swamps. Listen to the rustle of shells on the beach, see mullet leaping for the fun of life, watch the changing moods of rivers and lakes ruffled by changing winds.

Take time to see the night blooming cereus along the Indian River, century plants sending their seed stalks aspiring, the sea oats, black eyed Susans and "Candles of the Lord," those waxen-white yucca flowers on the dunes. Go out over the reef at John Pennekamp State Park in the Keys and look down through water clear as air at forests of living coral and sea plumes where jeweled fishes dart in and out of grottoes.

Take the by-ways, drop into quiet little towns where neon does not yet hide the stars, visit the Suwanee and the upper St. Johns, cruise up the St. Lucie or Loxahatchee.

Be able to say: "We saw the real Florida."

36

How to Understand the Animals

Up and down the reaches of the St. Lucie, in the saw grass swamps and the pine forests, where they had fed, lingered and loitered, the creatures were returning home at dawn before men should discover them.

Raccoons backed down from cabbage palm heads where they had feasted on the black berries. Opossums, otter and wildcats sought places to hide. The day is revealing and fearsome. Only the night is good, safe and comforting.

In the half-light, a little grey Florida fox came to the den where his vixen lay and placed a brown woods rat at its opening under the root of a fallen tree. He sat back on his haunches, red tongue lolling, until his mate came out, nipped him and chased him off before she seized the offering. Deep in the earth the kits cried and were only comforted when their mother brought them her milk again.

Early this day, in lordliness and majesty, the large diamondback rattlesnake moved on his belly up out of the dark of the gopher tortoise hole on the far side of the river where he had spent his last long sleep. He coiled a while to rest on the warm white sand which the land turtles had scooped out to pile before their den.

Like all the creatures, he lived in now, the ever present moment, this instant, this heartbeat, this slow, unnoticed breath and exhalation. He knew neither hours days nor years; his time was measured in hungers and satiations, in strange stirrings within. He lived at peace with the gopher turtles and the small ground owls, waxing thin or fat as other small creatures of the forest avoided him or blundered close. Sometimes he went for weeks without food until some luckless swamp rabbit crossed close by where he lurked and he touched it with his poisonous darts.

This was Spring, and as he lay coil upon coil at the mouth of the place where the turtles lived, his forked tongue darted and quivered. He who was so often the patient waiter by the side of the trail, was now restless, hungering for love.

He felt in his cold flesh, which the sun could never absolutely warm, his slow heart beating to a strange quickening. Gone was the time of the sleeper; this was the metamorphosis of wonder when he was to become the restless wanderer.

Just as twice each year he must shed the beautiful skin of his body, growing miraculously one more rattle upon his tail, so now he was seized with a strange madness not of his own making, to flow down the woods trails, cross the saw grass wastes and forests of spruce and pine, go over logs instead of around them, swim sloughs and cross rivers—for love.

In the heights, a graceful Everglades kite swooped and dived like a giant swallow, then came softly down to feed on an Everglades snail laying its eggs on a sedge stalk in a slough. The kite and its kind were tied to the snail and its kind by an invisible bond. As the snails dwindle through droughts, the kites become scarcer. They will eat no other food. Their kind hangs now on the edge of eternity.

To understand the animals, one must know that there are only these important things in life: food, safe shelter, a mate and progeny. The creatures and the plants, and most certainly ourselves, are mainly occupied with throwing the torch of our kinds forward in a ceaseless wave on the blue planet.

From the flat fly that lives in an osprey's feathers to midges dancing in a sunbeam, each is a self important to itself. The creatures are nameless and live in a world that is timeless, miraculous and unexplained. They are shaped to their wonders by millenia of adaptation, yet live in transient days and nights, without a speculative limbo behind or knowing of future unpleasantness ahead.

They get along fine without words, other than emotional sounds of warning, rage, fright, joy, satisfaction or provocation to terror. Most birds sing not for love but to protect their territorial rights.

The owl perches silent at dusk, then hoots and listens for the scurrying field mouse, the frightened meadow lark. It glides down on soft wings, seizes its prey in sharp talons and dismembers the mouse or bird for gaping owlets back at the nest. Cruelty is a sort of love. The frogs have me stumped. The most terrible sound in the cruel marsh is a leopard frog pleading for help when its foot is caught in the jaws of a snake. They exult, too. One night I got lost in Blue Cypress Swamp and the harder I tried to work my way out the deeper in I went, until at last just my head was sticking up out of the black swamp water in that awful dark.

It was a great night for frogs. They beeped and trilled, peeped and boomed, grunted and brayed in a mighty chorus up and down the St. Johns Marsh from Yeehaw clear to Holopaw. Frogs talk best when their enemies are in trouble, but whether what they say means anything is a matter open to doubt.

Possibly the animals do not need words to explain things. Try looking at anything long enough—label or none—and it begins to make sense just because it's here.

The animals are obsessed with enlightened self interest; no buck gives a hang what happens to the buck in the next neck of the woods. From their view, whatever is edible or lovable is good; if it hurts, it is bad.

Wouldn't it be a shock to discover that the animals are living in the world as it is, while ours is largely imaginary?

37
A Florida Cracker Came into His Own

There is no truth to the saying that you become a Florida Cracker after getting sand in your shoes. Not even being born in Florida since 1900 is enough. You may be a descendant of a pineapple planter, a fish house owner or someone who took President Grover Cleveland fishing–and that entitles you to join the Early Settlers Society. In the Keys, if great-grandpa was a wrecker, you are entitled to call yourself a Conch.

But Florida Cracker, no!

We have Georgia Crackers posing as Florida Crackers, but they are as dissimilar from the real thing as a pork chop is from a chunk of dried jerky.

Your dyed-in-the-wool, honest-to-God, genuine Florida Cracker traces his family back to the Indian Wars. Their folks were here when Colonel Zachary Taylor and his troops fought Chiefs Wildcat, Alligator and Sam Jones at the Battle of Okeechobee in 1837.

The Florida Cracker is as closely rooted to his pine and palmetto ranchland as the Tennessee mountaineer to his blue hills. He may rise to be a Supreme Court Justice or a Governor, but his heart stays at the ranch with his cows, catch-dogs and rattlesnakes.

His ancestors made their own salt from the sea, their own homespun from patches of cotton, ran wild hogs and wild cattle, lived off the land. The men were more at home on horseback than afoot. A man felt naked without his shotgun or rifle. Next to rounding up his wild cows (and a few of his neighbors' scrub cattle) to ship off to Cuba, he lived for the hunt. He fed his family on venison and wild turkey, sandhill cranes and wood storks. Except for fox squirrels big as a cat, which dwelt in the virgin yellow pine forests, he wouldn't waste powder on small critters such as ducks, quail, grey squirrels or rabbits.

If he really settled down, he lived in a square-built log cabin with a porch on four sides and a breezeway. All around the eaves of the porch would be the whitened skulls and antlers of the bucks he had killed to feed his family. Egret plumes, skinned-out alligator bellies, 'coon and otter hides were his money crops to trade for shot and powder or some fripperies for the women.

He was illiterate, but religious. There was always a family Bible in the home. Funerals were solemn events with home made coffins buried in the back yard. Occasionally a circuit rider came through and weddings were festive events, followed by fiddling and a square dance.

Your genuine Florida Cracker families have names

like Platts, Carlton, Rowell, Hendry, Bass, Cash, Alderman, Pearce and Whiddon. Some will tell you that they came to South Florida "when Great-Grandpa's Parson Browns got froze out at Fort Christmas in the 1880s." They migrated from places like Pine Level, Fort Meade, Fort Bassenger, Fort Drum, driving their wild cattle and hunting open range. They drove "seven-ox teams," hauling their family possessions from places like Paine's Prairie to settlements that lived on, like Indiantown and Fort Pierce.

They were grizzled, sunburned, taciturn folk, proud and self sufficient, quick to answer an insult, real or fancied. They were wind bitten and toil gnarled, with pale eyes squinched up from too much sun and neck skin as wrinkled as a turkey gobbler's. Even their children looked like they had been born freckled, sunburned and wind dried.

They were poor—but they are no more. Some of the die-hard families still own vast ranches in the Peace River Valley, Kissimmee Valley and Upper St. Johns Marsh and are worth millions in land and pure-bred cattle. They drive Jeeps but can afford Cadillacs and many have their own private planes. Their sons are among the leading attorneys, jurists, educators and businessmen in the state.

If a Cracker sells part of his ancestral land, he usually retains a few hundred acres around his home place for his personal enjoyment. We have one like that on the outskirts of our town. He sold enough land to developers to make himself a millionaire a couple of times over, fenced in the home acreage with "No Trespass!" signs every forty feet, and lived a happy life in the old style. He had an outhouse, a pitcher pump well by the kitchen door and tacked 'coon hides on the wall.

He would have done all right, except that his wife died, and instead of burying her in the yard he took her to town and had a church funeral.

While the services were going on, the sheriff and the State Beverage Department officers raided his still.

No real Florida Cracker would have ever done that.

38

The 'Possum War in the Back Yard Is an Exciting Event

Although we live in downtown Stuart, right spang in the heart of the settlement, we have been engaged in a war with the 'possums for the past several weeks. The 'possums are winning, which is all right with me. I sorta like 'em.

In fact, it all began with a mystery a couple of years ago. My daughter, engaging in culinary adventures, pulled out the bottom drawer of the oven where the pots and pans are stored and came running to me with word that "there's a big rat in the oven!"

I grabbed a small baseball bat and advanced on the open drawer. There, sleeping peacefully between a pie pan and a baking dish, eyes closed, a grin upon its face, was a small, grey opossum. It gave me a hiss or two as I raised it by its hairless tail, and deposited it in a croaker sack. I drove five miles out into the country, found a patch of woods that looked like it might

205

appeal to 'possums and shook the critter out of the bag.

The 'possum played dead for a minute, then rose on all fours, turned and gave me a certain look. I know now what the look was intended to convey. This was a town 'possum, not a country 'possum. Like MacArthur gazing back at Corregidor, it was saying "I will return."

For weeks the main subject of our family conversation was the great mystery: "How did the 'Possum get in the Oven?" My son was in the Army far away, so he couldn't have put it there; neither my daughter nor my wife would touch a 'possum with a ten-foot pole, so they were in the clear. We finally decided that the 'possum must have come down the chimney like Santa Claus, found the oven drawer open and crawled in to hibernate. Illogical—but like all other unexplained mysteries, the best we could do.

A year passed. One morning before breakfast I opened the back door and found Pudge, my big red dog, happily throwing a large limp ball of grey fur into the air and catching it as it came down. It was a full grown 'possum. Anyhow, I retrieved it, put it in a cardboard box where it revived rapidly, and then I took it on a fishing trip away on out back of Pratt and Whitney.

As I let it go in the boondocks, just on the chance that it was the same 'possum, I remarked "Indiantown is that way," pointing north, "and West Palm Beach that way," pointing south. The 'possum listened closely and started due northeast—toward Stuart.

Lots of things can happen on the way, I guess. Anyhow, we were 'possum-free until along about six

weeks ago when I heard a thump in the night on our
tin roof and then a series of smaller thumps, followed
by the patter of little feet.

It so happens that there is a hickory tree that spreads
its branches over one gable of our house and the
squirrels jump from it, run down the roof ridge and
jump on to a big mango tree that shades our back
porch. "Squirrels," I thought, "but isn't it unusual for
squirrels to be running around at night?"

In a few minutes, Pudge went wild. The dog's
eyeballs rolled, it huffed, puffed, ran wild scattering
rugs, and demanded to be let out the back door. Don't
think I ever saw Pudge get so excited. Fact of the
matter, the dog had been sort of listless, not eating all
of its food. We feed it outside the back steps.

So far as I know, Pudge has only one major hatred in
life and that is against any creature that dares to steal
left-over food. Kidnaping, bank robberies and all forms
of mayhem, in Pudge's book are nothing at all—but
steal so much as one left-over hushpuppy from that pan
under the mango tree and you have won a deadly
enemy for life.

So the war is on. The 'possums (note that I no longer
use the singular) come plumping on to the roof and
down the mango tree. Pudge chases them back up the
tree and has worn a deep groove of tracks around its
base.

At first it was a vociferous war, with the 'possums
making plenty of racket and the dog barking its head
off, but now both sides are resorting to strategy. The
'possums have taken to coming around at three or four
o'clock on these cold mornings; the dog tiptoes into my

bedroom and awakens me with the pat of a paw on my shoulder; I quietly open the back door and a red wolf with bared teeth slinks out.

Will we win? I doubt it. Early yesterday morning, shivering in my pajamas, I turned a powerful flashlight beam up into the mango tree and counted a great big 'possum and six little 'possums. We don't even open the oven drawers anymore.

39

Just a Glimmer of Kindness Is Showing in the Land

There are faint signs that we are moving toward a truce with the animals in this part of Florida. In the relentless war of men against everything else, little pockets of kindness are showing up.

It is still dangerous to pinpoint the exact locations where humankind is fraternizing with the enemy. The war is still too hot for that. But here are a few whiffs of the smell of peace, distant though it may be.

At a ranch home in the piney woods along about evening there is a regular visitor, a wild doe that timidly ventures into the yard and nibbles at slices of bread tendered by the ranch owner's wife. They have seen the buck watching from the distance but he has not yet gotten up the courage to believe that there is really a truce.

Instead of greeting them with bullets and selling their hides for leather, a few rivershore and lakeside dwellers have actually made friends with some alligators. They go down to the shore, call them in and feed them fish. It is particularly dangerous to be specific about where this occurs because 'gator hides are bringing $6 a foot and the poachers would hunt down the last one if they could find it.

There is a home far up one of the branches of the St. Lucie River where things have gone absolutely out of control. The residence has large sliding glass doors in its Florida room facing out upon a wooded clearing that leads down to the river, with jungle on both sides.

The man and the woman who reside in this lovely place have many hours of pleasure watching egrets returning to their roosts in the evening, herons fishing along the shore and quail, doves and squirrels feeding in their clearing. But lately the tables have been turned.

As they sat in their lighted home the other night, they got the oddest feeling that they were being watched. And they were! A little grey fox and a tawny spotted Florida wildcat were quietly sitting outside the glass doors, looking in.

Bird-watching and nature-watching in general have been increasing in popularity but it is distinctly a new trend when the animals start watching the people.

It is still unsafe to speculate on what this may lead to. It is extremely dangerous to make friends with any creature, because then you do not want to kill it or let anyone else do so.

This reporter regrets to announce that there have been a few isolated instances where Floridians have made friends with fish. Down in the Florida Keys, in a little grotto in the coral shoreline, a man has struck up acquaintance with several grouper to whom he makes gifts of the crawfish that they dearly love. The fish come to the surface, gulp crawfish and let him scratch their backs. How the crawfish regard this is another matter.

And up on the St. Johns River at a fishing camp, of all places, the proprietor walks out on the end of his pier with a bucket of shiners. He hits the dock three sharp raps, waves a shiner in the air, and the big black bass come from afar to be fed from his hands. This inconsiderate resort owner has posted signs: "No Fishing 1,000 Yds. from Dock."

All of this leads to the thought that if you know the lesser creatures a bit better it becomes more difficult to do them harm.

Perhaps the first step toward peace among men might be for more of us to know one another better.

40

St. Lucie Was *Rio De Luz,*
River of Light

One of the earliest Spanish maps of Florida shows the St. Lucie as *Rio de Luz*, the River of Light.

Our beautiful river also appears on ancient maps as *Rio de Santa Cruz*, the River of the Holy Cross. Historians say that it may have been so designated when Ponce de Leon deposited a cross of carved stone in the river to take possession in the name of Spain on his voyage southward from St. Augustine in 1513.

But they don't agree. Some hold that Ponce entered the Loxahatchee at Jupiter, where the Indians were so fierce that the Spaniards could not go ashore. They hold that the *Rio de Santa Cruz* application to the St. Lucie was because of the "geographical cross" where the channels of the St. Lucie and Indian River bisect each other opposite Rocky Point.

To heck with the historians. I like that name, River of Light, and isn't it logical that Lucea and Lucie might

215

have derived from Luz? In progression, the Spaniards called our stream *Santa Lucea* and the English Saint Lucie.

I like to think that some romantic Spanish explorer saw our river as I have seen it so many times, with the pink flush of dawn coming up from the sea dispelling the half-light, sweeping inland above the green tide, with a wave of light over the mangrove swamps, palm hammocks and pine forests.

The miracle of light upon a happy river in the morning is alchemy accepted, unexplained. The seabirds leave their roosts for the sea to dive and hover over the white puffs of striking fish. Up and ever up the river on the flooding tide come myriads of minnows with blues and ladyfish and mackerel slashing at their ranks.

Early in the morning the tarpon, the sea trout, snook and channel bass keep schools of mullet cascading and the brown pelicans come diving in to get their share. Porpoises leap and play, sigh and feed. In the early morning the bumbling manatee, like a small walrus without tusks, doe-eyed and inoffensive, propels herself upriver seeking a far and quiet place to bear her young.

Breezes ripple the face of the river and light glitters like tiny diamonds on the water. The sunlight paints golden trunks on the cabbage palms and accentuates the red crackled bark of the pines. The pine needles and the palm fronds are at last truly green again (whatever "green" is) and in the recesses of an upwater creek cascades of wild chrysanthemums are shining in unseen glory.

The advance of the light upstream on a tropical river is accompanied by those who advance and those who withdraw. The egrets leave their rookeries in undulating flight, the sandhill cranes stalk across the flatwoods with their cacophonic, rattling feeding call, the meadowlark perches on a wild honeysuckle and sings to the sun.

But the coming of light is also a coming of fear. The deer beds down in a hidden place and sleeps. The wildcat and the grey Florida fox seek hidden holes. The otter finds its den. For the hand of man is against these creatures and their lives are forfeit if they boldly roam in the day.

What a reflection it is upon the human race that most warm blooded wild creatures are creatures of the night. To them the light brings fear. They go "underground" in the beautiful day to survive the fiercest predator, ourselves.

Nor do the birds place any trust in us. Have you noticed that all of them have "distance tolerances?" So far and no farther may you approach before they're on the wing and it's usually just past the distance that shotgun pellets will carry.

Perhaps the St. Lucie should be called: "River of Light—and Fear."

41

Our Small Town Has Its Peculiarities

In Stuart, if you put on a coat you are going to church, a funeral or an installation. Add a hat and you are going to New York.

Here you get a friendly wave of the hand from everyone who knows you—and from many who don't. It's a place where you not only know your neighbors by their first names but also the names of their dogs, cats and parrakeets.

It's the sort of community where you can still carry on most business without any contract more formal than your word and the other fellow's.

You'd be amazed at how much chicken scratch our feed stores and chain stores sell to people who use it to feed wild birds and squirrels.

Several times in the past week we have noted automobile drivers *not* speeding up, *not* blaring their horns, but actually slowing to a stop and allowing pedestrians to cross East Ocean Boulevard.

And we understand that more and more fish are being given away, properly cleaned, pre-refrigerated and wrapped in wax paper.

Of course, there is that fellow over in the Bessey Addition who cranks up his gasoline powered lawn mower at 5:30 a.m. and jars the teeth out of everybody for two blocks around. Well, a man who would do that would shoplift, and anybody lowdown enough to steal will soon take to cashing bogus checks, is bound to be caught, and we'll be rid of him some day.

Stopped to chat with George Conrad at his filling station over by the tracks the other afternoon when a southbound train pulled in. The engineer waved at him, the conductor waved at him and a porter on the last car waved at him, and George waved back at all of them. Roused nostalgic memories of childhood when I waved at the engineer and he tooted his whistle, filling the backwoods with the most melodious sound on earth.

Speaking of the friendly salutation of the raised hand, it is still an almost universal custom upon the water. The fellow who can't take time to raise his hand when he passes another boat is in too much of a hurry to be enjoying life.

Plain old common courtesy even exists in the grim, no-quarter battle of chain store shopping. With my own eyes I saw a lady with a heaping full push-basket in the line behind the cashier turn to another behind her and with my own ears I heard her say: "You only have a few items, move in here in front of me."

We have the most courteous service station operators

in Florida, but they have a fiendish extra-sensory perception. When you have all day and are going nowhere, they gas you up, wave you on and jump to the next customer—but, if you are fifteen minutes late for a dinner appointment, they insist on checking your brake fluid, adding water to your battery and cleaning the windshield with tender loving care.

And it may be that it is sort of hard to get some of our doctors to make night calls. Not that I blame them, since we newspaper reporters detest night work almost as much.

Hope I wasn't rubbing it in when I told one of our esteemed medicos the yarn about the doctor who called up the plumber at 2 a.m. and yelled: "Get out here quick—the plumbing's stopped up and the bathroom is flooded—this is an emergency!" The plumber is said to have replied: "Just drop in a couple of aspirins and, if it isn't better by 9 a.m., call me up again."

Can't say that he enjoyed the joke but, at least, we're still on speaking terms, although he's calling me "Mister."

Nobody stays mad too long at anybody in a town where everybody is going to be seeing and rubbing shoulders with everyone else for the rest of their lives.

We may not all be related to each other in Stuart, but, with more than 100 civic, fraternal and religious organizations, it is hard to hold a good mad at somebody you are going to be sitting next to at church, eating with at Kiwanis, or expecting to get some work out of in the Chamber of Commerce committee of which you are chairman. Not to mention getting an item in the paper once in a while.

It is true that if you still find some of the men being extremely polite and calling each other "Mister" instead of by their first names, they haven't entirely gotten over being sore at each other.

But the reverse is true with the ladies. When they rush into each other's arms, inquire tenderly about the state of the opponent's health and say how much they have missed each other lately, the feud is still going strong.

I don't know which way is best. Personally, I'll settle for keeping on being called "Mister." Don't know that I could stand being slapped on the back and called by my first name by someone aching to poke me in the jaw.

42

How Beautiful Is My Home From on High

Home is where the heart is—even a mile or so in the sky—and I saw a picture of home the other day that I will never forget.

How beautiful our town is from on high!

The airliner seemed to pause high above the winding jungle river of the headwaters of the South Fork for me to drink in the beauty of the most beautiful part of the East Coast.

The Chamber of Commerce is not kidding you. The real estate men are not putting out any blarney. There is nothing else like it.

The afternoon was crystal clear and every detail of our marvelous panorama stood out in an unbelievable "aerial photograph in color."

There was the broad blue South Fork Bay stretching down past Palm City and the North Fork Bay coming down from St. Lucie Country Club, meeting at Stuart

223

and sweeping past our town to Port Sewall and the sea. The Indian River, Rio and Jensen Beach, Sewall's Point, the bridges, Hutchinson Island, St. Lucie Inlet and the blue Atlantic made a picture that tugged at my heartstrings.

I could make out the courthouse, The Stuart News building, my own home, and I felt a deep personal attachment for this town and its people. "That's my own home town," kept running through my mind, "where my friends live and where my wife is and my kinfolks and my dog–and where I make a living."

My feelings were even deeper than that, for I have been in Stuart a long, long time–and there were flashbacks of thought that could occur to no one but myself, personal memories of happiness connected with the geography.

The tiny coiled serpent of the South Fork reminded me of hundreds of days of happiness spent on the stream, from boyhood on. The inlet and the blue ocean gave me visions of hauling in king mackerel and blues and fighting sailfish. As we went over Mile Lake to the north, I saw a boy and his father catching bass with long cane poles using pork rind frogs for lures.

Looking down at St. Lucie Country Club, it seemed impossible that I had been inside that building a few nights before listening to a speech by the Secretary of Commerce of the United States.

Over Moonshine Bay on the North Fork, I recalled the happy evenings flycasting with Cap'n Flagg and Burt Pruitt–the thrill of an impossible tarpon which must have weighed 200 pounds, striking a plug on light bass tackle, breaking the line and leaping high over the boat. It had been absolutely incredible that such a fish could be played in close quarters on such tackle and we had laughed at the amazing encounter.

All the long way up to Pittsburgh, Pa., and all the long way back, I saw nothing in so beautiful a setting as my home – and I am an avid watcher-out-of-the-window.

My theory is that, as long as you've paid your fare you'd better get your money's worth, so I miss nothing: farms, thin lines of highways, the clusters of towns, hills, mountains, and cloud masses. Believe it or not, I even kept looking out when we were seven miles high and the holes through the clouds below were as blue as the sky above.

The new part of downtown Pittsburgh is striking in the modern architecture of towering aluminum and glass buildings and malls, but it isn't my home. Those rivers with the ore barges aren't my rivers, nor do the trees without leaves and the stark hills dusted with powdery snow belong in any way to me.

When I got back to the greenery, the warmth and the beauty of Stuart, I bored everyone by saying: "If you own anything here, don't sell it. Buy more."

Now I know why so many airline pilots, who have seen what I saw, pick this part of Florida for home. And why retired officers of the Army and the Navy have chosen this area for home after having been all over the world. We're lucky, lucky people to have a home like this.